Programed Ear Training   **VOLUME I: INTERVALS**

Programed Ear Training
Volume I: INTERVALS

Leo Horacek and Gerald Lefkoff
West Virginia University

Under the General Editorship of
Guy Alan Bockmon
University of Tennessee

HARCOURT, BRACE & WORLD, INC.

New York   Chicago   San Francisco   Atlanta

Library of Congress Catalog Number: 70-110129

Printed in the United States of America

Preface to the Instructor

PROGRAMED EAR TRAINING is designed to develop the hearing and notational skills required in the freshman and sophomore music theory courses. It consists of four programed workbooks and accompanying tape recordings that provide a complete course of study in melodic and harmonic dictation, sightsinging, and aural harmonic analysis. The four volumes are:

     I. INTERVALS
    II. MELODY AND RHYTHM
   III. CHORDS, Part I
   IV. CHORDS, Part II

The flexibility of the program makes it suitable for use in any kind of theory program. The volumes may be used singly or as a group, alone or in combination with other text materials. Except for Volume IV, which depends on Volume III, they need not be taken sequentially; experience has shown, in fact, that for some students it is more profitable to work in several volumes concurrently.

Because the course is programed, the student works entirely on his own, at his own pace. Multiple copies of each written lesson are provided, so that he can repeat lessons as often as necessary to improve his skills. As he reaches recommended levels of proficiency, he takes tests, which are provided separately to the instructor and administered under his direction. A guide to the administration and grading of the program is provided in the Instructor's Manual.

PROGRAMED EAR TRAINING was developed at West Virginia University over a seven-year period during which it was in continuous use and was constantly being revised. It has also been used at more than a dozen other colleges and universities across the country; thus it has been thoroughly tested with large and varying groups of students.

The authors would like to express appreciation to Dr. Guy Bockmon, University of Tennessee, for his careful reading of all the materials and for his most helpful recommendations; to Dr. Richard E. Duncan, Dean of the Creative Arts Center, West Virginia University, who suggested and supported the project in which these books were developed; to Dr. Frank Lorince, Chairman of the Theory Department, West Virginia University, for his valuable advice and assistance; to the teachers who have used the books and offered suggestions and criticism; and finally to the many students who have worked patiently or otherwise through the program and whose reactions were always useful.

L.H.
G.L.

Contents

INTRODUCTION

This is the first of four volumes designed to help you improve your hearing and notational skills through the techniques of programed instruction. Volume I is devoted to intervals. The first four series of lessons are designed to improve your skills in hearing, singing, and notating melodic intervals; the last three series provide practice in hearing and notating harmonic intervals. For each lesson in the program there is a tape recording that provides all the audio material you will need to complete the lesson.

Programed instruction differs from usual instruction in two ways: first, most of the work can be done with little or no help from a teacher; and second, you can progress at your own rate. Where the material is difficult, you can move slowly. Where you find it easy, you can move rapidly, saving time and work. A faculty advisor will probably direct and guide your work, but the responsibility for making progress is yours. Through your test scores and your scores on each lesson, you will always know how well you are progressing.

The basic idea of programed instruction is as follows. The material to be learned is broken into small units called *frames*. In each frame, a small problem is presented and you will be asked to make a response. Immediately after this response, the correct answer is provided so that you will know whether or not your response was correct. Through many confirmations of correct responses and corrections of incorrect responses, complicated and difficult skills and concepts can be learned with ease. With the programed instruction procedures in this book, you will find that you can spend as little or as much time in any one area as you need.

For each lesson a goal has been set for you, to show you whether you are ready to move on to the next lesson. If you complete a lesson with no more than the number of errors indicated in the goal, move on to the next lesson. Otherwise you are to repeat the lesson. For this purpose five copies of every worksheet are provided (except for the sightsinging lessons). If after five tries you have not brought the number of errors down to the limit set in the goal, move on to the next lesson anyway.

When you have completed the entire series in this fashion, take the test on that series. You will take the tests on your own, but they will be graded by your instructor. The score you will receive on each test is a *weighted score*, which means that your raw score is multiplied by a factor to compensate for the length, difficulty, and importance of the series.

The evaluation of your work will depend on the total of all your test scores rather than on an average of these scores. Therefore every test you take, even if the score is low, can help raise your grade. If you return to a series for more work in that area, you may retake the test and count the highest grade you make on that test. To help you know how well you are doing, three *achievement levels* are provided for each test.

The *first level* represents a very high degree of learning. Generally, when you have achieved this level you should not plan to return to the material in the series but should spend your time on other material.

The *second level* represents a moderate achievement. The material in the series can be considered to be reasonably well learned, but if time permits or if you wish to raise your grade, it would be practical to return to the series for further work.

The *third level* represents a rather low but nevertheless significant amount of learning. You should at some time return to the series for further work.

Normally it is most advantageous to move on from one series to the next regardless of the test scores, and then at certain points in the course go back and do further work on any series on which your test score was lower than you would like. The most profitable pattern of moving on and working back varies from student to student, and it will be best to seek the advice of your instructor when you are undecided.

The *test record sheet* that appears at the end of this volume indicates for each test the three achievement levels and the maximum possible score, and provides a convenient place to keep a record of your scores.

The skills developed through this course of study are extremely valuable in almost any musical activity. Not only are they important in performing music, but they can also help you to understand music you hear, to arrange and write music, and to discuss and learn more about music.

With the method of study used in these volumes, you will find that you can work to develop these skills in the manner best suited to your particular needs and abilities. You can move slowly where you find difficulties, change to a different part of the course if your progress has slowed down, and work at maximum speed where your competencies are strongest. This modern approach to music theory can enable you to learn these important skills in the most efficient manner possible.

Melodic Interval Discrimination SERIES A1

The purpose of this series is to develop your ability to recognize the sounds of various intervals of different size. In each lesson, the task is to discriminate, from all the intervals heard, those of a particular size.

The two notes that make up the intervals heard in this series are presented in melodic fashion; that is, they are heard one after the other. Such intervals are called melodic intervals.

After each interval you hear on the tape, there is a very brief pause during which you are to decide whether the interval that you have just heard is the one you have been asked to discriminate. If you think it is, make a tally mark on a piece of paper. If you think it is not, do not make a mark. If the interval was the particular interval you are to discriminate, you will hear a high-pitched electronic signal. If you do not hear the electronic signal, you will know it was some other interval.

Thus your answer will be correct 1) if you make a tally mark and then hear the electronic signal, or 2) if you *do not* make a mark and *do not* hear the signal. You may think of your task as that of trying to make a tally mark before and only before each electronic signal is heard.

Printed answer sheets are not needed for these lessons. Any sheet of blank paper can be used for your responses. Make your tally marks in groups of five in a single row as long as your responses are correct. If you make an error, begin a new line. Your paper will then look something like this:

```
I I I I
I
||||I  I I
I I I
||||I  ||||I  ||||I
```

Your goal is to achieve one line with fifteen tally marks. As soon as you do, go on to the next lesson. You need not go to the end of the lesson after you have reached that goal. If you do not attain the goal by the end of the lesson, repeat the lesson until you do or until you have been through the lesson five times, at which point you should go on to the next lesson regardless of your score.

The discrimination interval for each lesson in this series is as follows:

A1-1	minor second
A1-2	major second

A1–3	minor third
A1–4	major third
A1–5	perfect fourth
A1–6	tritone
A1–7	perfect fifth
A1–8	minor sixth
A1–9	major sixth
A1–10	minor seventh
A1–11	major seventh
A1–12	perfect octave

The lessons may be done in any order. It is convenient to do them in the above order, but if the tape you need is in use, do another lesson.

There is no test for this series. While your achievement in melodic interval discrimination is not tested, this skill will help you in the series that follow, for which there are tests.

Interval Sightsinging   SERIES A2

The purpose of this series is to develop the ability to sing the pitches of an interval written in staff notation. A printed worksheet and a tape recording are provided for each lesson. The frames on the worksheet are separated by bar lines. Each contains two notes. The corresponding material on the tape recording has the following format: a tone will give the pitch of the first note, followed by two clicks of a metronome. You are to sing the two notes along with these two clicks. Immediately after the clicks two tones will give the pitches you should have sung. You can then judge if you sang the printed notes correctly.

Depending on the range of your voice, you may find it necessary to sing in a different octave from that of the tones you hear on the tape recording. You may also find it necessary to change octaves in the course of a lesson. Sing in the most comfortable part of your vocal range at all times.

Whenever you have not sung a complete frame correctly, make a tally mark on a piece of paper. Your goal is to complete each lesson with no more than twelve errors. When you have done so, go on to the next lesson. If you have made more than twelve errors, repeat the lesson until you reach the goal or until you have done the lesson five times, at which point you should go on to the next lesson regardless of your score.

The first seven lessons in this series (A2–1 to A2–7) are written in the treble clef. The last two lessons (A2–8 and A2–9) are written in the bass clef. There are two tests for this series. Test A2a is a test in sightsinging intervals in the treble clef and should be taken following lesson A2–7. Test A2b is a test in sightsinging intervals in the bass clef and should be taken following lesson A2–9.

A2-1 Interval sightsinging: Major and minor seconds

Listen to the first tone of the frame, sing both tones, and compare your response with the tape. Tally errors on a separate sheet of paper. Goal: No more than twelve errors.

A2-2 Interval sightsinging: Major and minor thirds

Listen to the first tone of the frame, sing both tones, and compare your response with the tape. Tally errors on a separate sheet of paper. Goal: No more than twelve errors.

A2-3 Interval sightsinging: Perfect and augmented fourths, perfect and diminished fifths

Listen to the first tone of the frame, sing both tones, and compare your response with the tape. Tally errors on a separate sheet of paper. Goal: No more than twelve errors.

A2-4 Interval sightsinging: Major and minor sixths

Listen to the first tone of the frame, sing both tones, and compare your response with the tape. Tally errors on a separate sheet of paper. Goal: No more than twelve errors.

9

A2-5 Interval sightsinging: Major and minor sevenths, perfect octaves

Listen to the first tone of the frame, sing both tones, and compare your response with the tape. Tally errors on a separate sheet of paper. Goal: No more than twelve errors.

A2-6 Interval sightsinging: All intervals previously studied

Listen to the first tone of the frame, sing both tones, and compare your response with the tape. Tally errors on a separate sheet of paper. Goal: No more than twelve errors.

A2-7 Interval sightsinging: All intervals previously studied

Listen to the first tone of the frame, sing both tones, and compare your response with the tape. Tally errors separately. Goal: No more than twelve errors. After you have done this lesson, take Test A2a.

A2-8 Interval sightsinging: All intervals previously studied

Listen to the first tone of the frame, sing both tones, and compare your response with the tape. Tally errors on a separate sheet of paper. Goal: No more than twelve errors.

A2-9 Interval sightsinging: All intervals previously studied

Listen to the first tone of the frame, sing both tones, and compare your response with the tape. Tally errors separately. Goal: No more than twelve errors. After you have done this lesson, take Test A2b.

Melodic Interval Dictation SERIES A3

The purpose of this series is to develop your ability to write melodic intervals that you hear. A printed worksheet and a tape recording are provided for each lesson. The frames on the worksheet are separated by bar lines. At the beginning of each frame you will find a note that corresponds to the first tone of the melodic interval you will hear on the tape recording. At the end of the frame you will find a small note that corresponds to the second tone of the interval.

To do each frame, start by shielding the small note at the end of the frame with a piece of paper or a card. After you have heard the two tones of the interval, write the second note of the interval in the space before the shield. Then slide the shield to the right and compare the note you have written with the small note you have uncovered. Your response is correct if the note you have written is the same as the small note or *enharmonic* with it. (Two notes are said to be enharmonic when they refer to the same pitch: for example, F sharp and G flat.) Circle each frame in which your response is incorrect. You may stop the tape occasionally if you need more time, but before going on to the next lesson, you should be able to complete the lesson without stopping.

Your goal is to complete each lesson with no more than twelve errors. When you have done so, go on to the next lesson. If you have made more than twelve errors, repeat the lesson until you reach the goal or until you have done the lesson five times, at which point you should go on to the next lesson regardless of your score.

The first seven lessons of this series (A3–1 to A3–7) are written in the treble clef. The last two lessons (A3–8 and A3–9) are written in the bass clef. There are two tests for this series. Test A3a is a test in melodic interval dictation in the treble clef and should be taken following lesson A3–7. Test A3b is a test in melodic interval dictation in the bass clef and should be taken following lesson A3–9.

A3-1
(Copy 1)

Melodic interval dictation: Major and minor seconds

Shield the answer. Listen to the interval and notate the second tone; then uncover the answer and compare your response. Circle incorrect responses. Goal: No more than twelve errors.

A3-1 Melodic interval dictation: Major and minor seconds
(Copy 2)

Shield the answer. Listen to the interval and notate the second tone; then uncover the answer and compare your response. Circle incorrect responses. Goal: No more than twelve errors.

A3-1 Melodic interval dictation: Major and minor seconds
(Copy 3)

Shield the answer. Listen to the interval and notate the second tone; then uncover the answer and compare your response. Circle incorrect responses. Goal: No more than twelve errors.

A3-1

Melodic interval dictation: Major and minor seconds

Shield the answer. Listen to the interval and notate the second tone; then uncover the answer and compare your response. Circle incorrect responses. Goal: No more than twelve errors.

19

A3-1

Melodic interval dictation: Major and minor seconds

Shield the answer. Listen to the interval and notate the second tone; then uncover the answer and compare your response. Circle incorrect responses. Goal: No more than twelve errors.

20

A3-2

(Copy 1)

Melodic interval dictation: Major and minor thirds

Shield the answer. Listen to the interval and notate the second tone; then uncover the answer and compare your response. Circle incorrect responses. Goal: No more than twelve errors.

21

A3-2
(Copy 2)

Melodic interval dictation: Major and minor thirds

Shield the answer. Listen to the interval and notate the second tone; then uncover the answer and compare your response. Circle incorrect responses. Goal: No more than twelve errors.

A3-2 Melodic interval dictation: Major and minor thirds

Shield the answer. Listen to the interval and notate the second tone; then uncover the answer and compare your response. Circle incorrect responses. Goal: No more than twelve errors.

A3-2

Melodic interval dictation: Major and minor thirds

(Copy 4)

Shield the answer. Listen to the interval and notate the second tone; then uncover the answer and compare your response. Circle incorrect responses. Goal: No more than twelve errors.

A3-2
(Copy 5)

Melodic interval dictation: Major and minor thirds

Shield the answer. Listen to the interval and notate the second tone; then uncover the answer and compare your response. Circle incorrect responses. Goal: No more than twelve errors.

A3-3

Melodic interval dictation: Perfect and augmented fourths, perfect and diminished fifths

Shield the answer. Listen to the interval and notate the second tone; then uncover the answer and compare your response. Circle incorrect responses. Goal: No more than twelve errors.

26

A3-3
(Copy 2)

Melodic interval dictation: Perfect and augmented fourths, perfect and diminished fifths

Shield the answer. Listen to the interval and notate the second tone; then uncover the answer and compare your response. Circle incorrect responses. Goal: No more than twelve errors.

A3-3
(Copy 3)

Melodic interval dictation: Perfect and augmented fourths, perfect and diminished fifths

Shield the answer. Listen to the interval and notate the second tone; then uncover the answer and compare your response. Circle incorrect responses. Goal: No more than twelve errors.

A3-3
Melodic interval dictation: Perfect and augmented fourths, perfect and diminished fifths

Shield the answer. Listen to the interval and notate the second tone; then uncover the answer and compare your response. Circle incorrect responses. Goal: No more than twelve errors.

29

Melodic interval dictation: Perfect and augmented fourths, perfect and diminished fifths

Shield the answer. Listen to the interval and notate the second tone; then uncover the answer and compare your response. Circle incorrect responses. Goal: No more than twelve errors.

A3-4

(Copy 1)

Melodic interval dictation: Major and minor sixths

Shield the answer. Listen to the interval and notate the second tone; then uncover the answer and compare your response. Circle incorrect responses. Goal: No more than twelve errors.

31

A3-4
(Copy 2)

Melodic interval dictation: Major and minor sixths

Shield the answer. Listen to the interval and notate the second tone; then uncover the answer and compare your response. Circle incorrect responses. Goal: No more than twelve errors.

A3-4 Melodic interval dictation: Major and minor sixths

(Copy 3)

Shield the answer. Listen to the interval and notate the second tone; then uncover the answer and compare your response. Circle incorrect responses. Goal: No more than twelve errors.

A3-4 Melodic interval dictation: Major and minor sixths

(Copy 4)

Shield the answer. Listen to the interval and notate the second tone; then uncover the answer and compare your response. Circle incorrect responses. Goal: No more than twelve errors.

A3-4

Melodic interval dictation: Major and minor sixths

Shield the answer. Listen to the interval and notate the second tone; then uncover the answer and compare your response. Circle incorrect responses. Goal: No more than twelve errors.

35

A3-5
(Copy 1)

Melodic interval dictation: Major and minor sevenths, perfect octaves

Shield the answer. Listen to the interval and notate the second tone; then uncover the answer and compare your response. Circle incorrect responses. Goal: No more than twelve errors.

A3-5

Melodic interval dictation: Major and minor sevenths, perfect octaves

Shield the answer. Listen to the interval and notate the second tone; then uncover the answer and compare your response. Circle incorrect responses. Goal: No more than twelve errors.

37

A3-5
(Copy 3)

Melodic interval dictation: Major and minor sevenths, perfect octaves

Shield the answer. Listen to the interval and notate the second tone; then uncover the answer and compare your response. Circle incorrect responses. Goal: No more than twelve errors.

A3-5 Melodic interval dictation: Major and minor sevenths, perfect octaves
(Copy 4)

Shield the answer. Listen to the interval and notate the second tone; then uncover the answer and compare your response. Circle incorrect responses. Goal: No more than twelve errors.

39

A3-5
(Copy 5)

Melodic interval dictation: Major and minor sevenths, perfect octaves

Shield the answer. Listen to the interval and notate the second tone; then uncover the answer and compare your response. Circle incorrect responses. Goal: No more than twelve errors.

A3-6

Melodic interval dictation: All intervals previously studied

Shield the answer. Listen to the interval and notate the second tone; then uncover the answer and compare your response. Circle incorrect responses. Goal: No more than twelve errors.

41

A3-6
(Copy 2)

Melodic interval dictation: All intervals previously studied

Shield the answer. Listen to the interval and notate the second tone; then uncover the answer and compare your response. Circle incorrect responses. Goal: No more than twelve errors.

42

A3-6

Melodic interval dictation: All intervals previously studied

Shield the answer. Listen to the interval and notate the second tone; then uncover the answer and compare your response. Circle incorrect responses. Goal: No more than twelve errors.

A3-6

(Copy 4)

Melodic interval dictation: All intervals previously studied

Shield the answer. Listen to the interval and notate the second tone; then uncover the answer and compare your response. Circle incorrect responses. Goal: No more than twelve errors.

A3-6

Melodic interval dictation: All intervals previously studied

(Copy 5)

Shield the answer. Listen to the interval and notate the second tone; then uncover the answer and compare your response. Circle incorrect responses. Goal: No more than twelve errors.

A3-7
(Copy 1)

Melodic interval dictation: All intervals previously studied

Shield the answer. Listen to the interval and notate the second tone; then check your response. Circle incorrect responses. Goal: No more than twelve errors. After you have done this lesson, take Test A3a.

A3-7 Melodic interval dictation: All intervals previously studied

(Copy 2)

Shield the answer. Listen to the interval and notate the second tone; then check your response. Circle incorrect responses. Goal: No more than twelve errors. After you have done this lesson, take Test A3a.

A3-7
(Copy 3)

Melodic interval dictation: All intervals previously studied

Shield the answer. Listen to the interval and notate the second tone; then check your response. Circle incorrect responses. Goal: No more than twelve errors. After you have done this lesson, take Test A3a.

A3-7

Melodic interval dictation: All intervals previously studied

Shield the answer. Listen to the interval and notate the second tone; then check your response. Circle incorrect responses. Goal: No more than twelve errors. After you have done this lesson, take Test A3a.

49

Melodic interval dictation: All intervals previously studied

Shield the answer. Listen to the interval and notate the second tone; then check your response. Circle incorrect responses. Goal: No more than twelve errors. After you have done this lesson, take Test A3a.

A3-8

(Copy 1)

Melodic interval dictation: All intervals previously studied

Shield the answer. Listen to the interval and notate the second tone; then uncover the answer and compare your response. Circle incorrect responses. Goal: No more than twelve errors.

A3-8
(Copy 2)

Melodic interval dictation: All intervals previously studied

Shield the answer. Listen to the interval and notate the second tone; then uncover the answer and compare your response. Circle incorrect responses. Goal: No more than twelve errors.

52

A3-8
(Copy 3)

Melodic interval dictation: All intervals previously studied

Shield the answer. Listen to the interval and notate the second tone; then uncover the answer and compare your response. Circle incorrect responses. Goal: No more than twelve errors.

A3-8

(Copy 4)

Melodic interval dictation: All intervals previously studied

Shield the answer. Listen to the interval and notate the second tone; then uncover the answer and compare your response. Circle incorrect responses. Goal: No more than twelve errors.

A3-8

Melodic interval dictation: All intervals previously studied

Shield the answer. Listen to the interval and notate the second tone; then uncover the answer and compare your response. Circle incorrect responses. Goal: No more than twelve errors.

55

A3-9

(Copy 1)

Melodic interval dictation: All intervals previously studied

Shield the answer. Listen to the interval and notate the second tone; then check your response. Circle incorrect responses. Goal: No more than twelve errors. After you have done this lesson, take Test A3b.

A3-9

(Copy 2)

Melodic interval dictation: All intervals previously studied

Shield the answer. Listen to the interval and notate the second tone; then check your response. Circle incorrect responses. Goal: No more than twelve errors. After you have done this lesson, take Test A3b.

A3-9

(Copy 3)

Melodic interval dictation: All intervals previously studied

Shield the answer. Listen to the interval and notate the second tone; then check your response. Circle incorrect responses. Goal: No more than twelve errors. After you have done this lesson, take Test A3b.

58

Melodic interval dictation: All intervals previously studied

Shield the answer. Listen to the interval and notate the second tone; then check your response. Circle incorrect responses. Goal: No more than twelve errors. After you have done this lesson, take Test A3b.

A3-9 Melodic interval dictation: All intervals previously studied
(Copy 5)

Shield the answer. Listen to the interval and notate the second tone; then check your response. Circle incorrect responses. Goal: No more than twelve errors. After you have done this lesson, take Test A3b.

Melodic Interval Identification **SERIES A4**

The purpose of this series is to develop your ability to identify the size of intervals that you hear. The following set of symbols will be used to identify the intervals:

−2 minor second	5 perfect fifth
2 major second	−6 minor sixth
−3 minor third	6 major sixth
3 major third	−7 minor seventh
4 perfect fourth	7 major seventh
T tritone	8 perfect octave

Thus the symbols for minor intervals consist of a minus sign and an Arabic numeral, and those for major and perfect intervals consist of only an Arabic numeral. You may think of the latter symbols as containing a blank and a numeral, the blank indicating that the interval is either major or perfect. The symbol T stands for the tritone, the interval that is written in two ways: as an augmented fourth or as a diminished fifth.

A printed worksheet and a tape recording are provided for each lesson. Each frame contains a blank followed by the correct answer. Start by covering the answer with a shield. When you have heard the interval, write the symbol for it in the blank; then slide the shield to the right and check your response. Circle the frame if your response is incorrect. Work across the page from left to right. You may stop the tape occasionally if you need more time, but before going on to the next lesson, you should be able to complete the lesson without stopping.

Your goal is to complete each lesson with no more than twelve errors. When you have done so, go on to the next lesson. If you have made more than twelve errors, repeat the lesson until you reach the goal or until you have done the lesson five times, at which point you should go on to the next lesson regardless of your score.

There is one test for this series, to be taken following lesson A4-7.

A4-1
(Copy 1)

Melodic interval identification: Major and minor seconds and thirds

Shield the answer. Listen to the interval and write 2, −2, 3, or −3 in the blank; then uncover the answer and compare your response. Circle incorrect responses. Goal: No more than twelve errors.

1   ___ −2   ___ 2   ___ −3   ___ 3   ___ 2   ___ 3   ___ −2   ___ −3

2   ___ 2   ___ −2   ___ −3   ___ 2   ___ 3   ___ −2   ___ −3   ___ 3

3   ___ −2   ___ 2   ___ −2   ___ −3   ___ 3   ___ 2   ___ −3   ___ −2

4   ___ −2   ___ 2   ___ 3   ___ −3   ___ 3   ___ −3   ___ 2   ___ 3

5   ___ −3   ___ 3   ___ −2   ___ 2   ___ −3   ___ −2   ___ 3   ___ 2

6   ___ 3   ___ 2   ___ −3   ___ −2   ___ 3   ___ −3   ___ 2   ___ −2

7   ___ −2   ___ −2   ___ 2   ___ 2   ___ −3   ___ 3   ___ 3   ___ −3

8   ___ 2   ___ −2   ___ 3   ___ 2   ___ −3   ___ −3   ___ −2   ___ 3

9   ___ −2   ___ 2   ___ 2   ___ 3   ___ −3   ___ −3   ___ 3   ___ −2

10   ___ −3   ___ 3   ___ 3   ___ −3   ___ −3   ___ 3   ___ 3   ___ −3

11   ___ 2   ___ −2   ___ −3   ___ 3   ___ −3   ___ 3   ___ −3   ___ 2

12   ___ −3   ___ 3   ___ −2   ___ 2   ___ −3   ___ −2   ___ 2   ___ −2

A4-1
(Copy 2)

Melodic interval identification: Major and minor seconds and thirds

Shield the answer. Listen to the interval and write 2, −2, 3, or −3 in the blank; then uncover the answer and compare your response. Circle incorrect responses. Goal: No more than twelve errors.

1   ___ −2   ___ 2   ___ −3   ___ 3   ___ 2   ___ 3   ___ −2   ___ −3

2   ___ 2   ___ −2   ___ −3   ___ 2   ___ 3   ___ −2   ___ −3   ___ 3

3   ___ −2   ___ 2   ___ −2   ___ −3   ___ 3   ___ 2   ___ −3   ___ −2

4   ___ −2   ___ 2   ___ 3   ___ −3   ___ 3   ___ −3   ___ 2   ___ 3

5   ___ −3   ___ 3   ___ −2   ___ 2   ___ −3   ___ −2   ___ 3   ___ 2

6   ___ 3   ___ 2   ___ −3   ___ −2   ___ 3   ___ −3   ___ 2   ___ −2

7   ___ −2   ___ −2   ___ 2   ___ 2   ___ −3   ___ 3   ___ 3   ___ −3

8   ___ 2   ___ −2   ___ 3   ___ 2   ___ −3   ___ −3   ___ −2   ___ 3

9   ___ −2   ___ 2   ___ 2   ___ 3   ___ −3   ___ −3   ___ 3   ___ −2

10   ___ −3   ___ 3   ___ 3   ___ −3   ___ −3   ___ 3   ___ 3   ___ −3

11   ___ 2   ___ −2   ___ −3   ___ 3   ___ −3   ___ 3   ___ −3   ___ 2

12   ___ −3   ___ 3   ___ −2   ___ 2   ___ −3   ___ −2   ___ 2   ___ −2

A4-1
(Copy 3)

Melodic interval identification: Major and minor seconds and thirds

Shield the answer. Listen to the interval and write 2, −2, 3, or −3 in the blank; then uncover the answer and compare your response. Circle incorrect responses. Goal: No more than twelve errors.

1 ____ −2 ____ 2 ____ −3 ____ 3 ____ 2 ____ 3 ____ −2 ____ −3

2 ____ 2 ____ −2 ____ −3 ____ 2 ____ 3 ____ −2 ____ −3 ____ 3

3 ____ −2 ____ 2 ____ −2 ____ −3 ____ 3 ____ 2 ____ −3 ____ −2

4 ____ −2 ____ 2 ____ 3 ____ −3 ____ 3 ____ −3 ____ 2 ____ 3

5 ____ −3 ____ 3 ____ −2 ____ 2 ____ −3 ____ −2 ____ 3 ____ 2

6 ____ 3 ____ 2 ____ −3 ____ −2 ____ 3 ____ −3 ____ 2 ____ −2

7 ____ −2 ____ −2 ____ 2 ____ 2 ____ −3 ____ 3 ____ 3 ____ −3

8 ____ 2 ____ −2 ____ 3 ____ 2 ____ −3 ____ −3 ____ −2 ____ 3

9 ____ −2 ____ 2 ____ 2 ____ 3 ____ −3 ____ −3 ____ 3 ____ −2

10 ____ −3 ____ 3 ____ 3 ____ −3 ____ −3 ____ 3 ____ 3 ____ −3

11 ____ 2 ____ −2 ____ −3 ____ 3 ____ −3 ____ 3 ____ −3 ____ 2

12 ____ −3 ____ 3 ____ −2 ____ 2 ____ −3 ____ −2 ____ 2 ____ −2

A4-1
(Copy 4)

Melodic interval identification: Major and minor seconds and thirds

Shield the answer. Listen to the interval and write 2, −2, 3, or −3 in the blank; then uncover the answer and compare your response. Circle incorrect responses. Goal: No more than twelve errors.

1 ____ −2 ____ 2 ____ −3 ____ 3 ____ 2 ____ 3 ____ −2 ____ −3

2 ____ 2 ____ −2 ____ −3 ____ 2 ____ 3 ____ −2 ____ −3 ____ 3

3 ____ −2 ____ 2 ____ −2 ____ −3 ____ 3 ____ 2 ____ −3 ____ −2

4 ____ −2 ____ 2 ____ 3 ____ −3 ____ 3 ____ −3 ____ 2 ____ 3

5 ____ −3 ____ 3 ____ −2 ____ 2 ____ −3 ____ −2 ____ 3 ____ 2

6 ____ 3 ____ 2 ____ −3 ____ −2 ____ 3 ____ −3 ____ 2 ____ −2

7 ____ −2 ____ −2 ____ 2 ____ 2 ____ −3 ____ 3 ____ 3 ____ −3

8 ____ 2 ____ −2 ____ 3 ____ 2 ____ −3 ____ −3 ____ −2 ____ 3

9 ____ −2 ____ 2 ____ 2 ____ 3 ____ −3 ____ −3 ____ 3 ____ −2

10 ____ −3 ____ 3 ____ 3 ____ −3 ____ −3 ____ 3 ____ 3 ____ −3

11 ____ 2 ____ −2 ____ −3 ____ 3 ____ −3 ____ 3 ____ −3 ____ 2

12 ____ −3 ____ 3 ____ −2 ____ 2 ____ −3 ____ −2 ____ 2 ____ −2

A4–1
(Copy 5)

Melodic interval identification: Major and minor seconds and thirds

Shield the answer. Listen to the interval and write 2, −2, 3, or −3 in the blank; then uncover the answer and compare your response. Circle incorrect responses. Goal: No more than twelve errors.

1 ___ −2 ___ 2 ___ −3 ___ 3 ___ 2 ___ 3 ___ −2 ___ −3

2 ___ 2 ___ −2 ___ −3 ___ 2 ___ 3 ___ −2 ___ −3 ___ 3

3 ___ −2 ___ 2 ___ −2 ___ −3 ___ 3 ___ 2 ___ −3 ___ −2

4 ___ −2 ___ 2 ___ 3 ___ −3 ___ 3 ___ −3 ___ 2 ___ 3

5 ___ −3 ___ 3 ___ −2 ___ 2 ___ −3 ___ −2 ___ 3 ___ 2

6 ___ 3 ___ 2 ___ −3 ___ −2 ___ 3 ___ −3 ___ 2 ___ −2

7 ___ −2 ___ −2 ___ 2 ___ 2 ___ −3 ___ 3 ___ 3 ___ −3

8 ___ 2 ___ −2 ___ 3 ___ 2 ___ −3 ___ −3 ___ −2 ___ 3

9 ___ −2 ___ 2 ___ 2 ___ 3 ___ −3 ___ −3 ___ 3 ___ −2

10 ___ −3 ___ 3 ___ 3 ___ −3 ___ −3 ___ 3 ___ 3 ___ −3

11 ___ 2 ___ −2 ___ −3 ___ 3 ___ −3 ___ 3 ___ −3 ___ 2

12 ___ −3 ___ 3 ___ −2 ___ 2 ___ −3 ___ −2 ___ 2 ___ −2

64

A4-2
(Copy 1)

Melodic interval identification: Major thirds, perfect fourths and fifths, tritones

Shield the answer. Listen to the interval and write 3, 4, 5, or T in the blank; then uncover the answer and compare your response. Circle incorrect responses. Goal: No more than twelve errors.

1 ___ 4 ___ 5 ___ T ___ 4 ___ 3 ___ 4 ___ 5 ___ 4
2 ___ 4 ___ 4 ___ 4 ___ 5 ___ 4 ___ 5 ___ 4 ___ 5
3 ___ 4 ___ 5 ___ 3 ___ 4 ___ T ___ 5 ___ 4 ___ 5
4 ___ 4 ___ 4 ___ 4 ___ 5 ___ 4 ___ 5 ___ 4 ___ 5
5 ___ 5 ___ 4 ___ 5 ___ 4 ___ 4 ___ 5 ___ 5 ___ 4
6 ___ 5 ___ 4 ___ 4 ___ 5 ___ 5 ___ 4 ___ 5 ___ 5
7 ___ 5 ___ 3 ___ 4 ___ T ___ 5 ___ 5 ___ T ___ 4
8 ___ 3 ___ 4 ___ 5 ___ T ___ 5 ___ 4 ___ 3 ___ 4
9 ___ 4 ___ 4 ___ 5 ___ 4 ___ T ___ 5 ___ 4 ___ T
10 ___ 5 ___ 4 ___ T ___ 5 ___ 5 ___ 4 ___ T ___ 5
11 ___ 5 ___ 4 ___ 3 ___ 4 ___ T ___ 4 ___ T ___ 4
12 ___ 5 ___ 5 ___ T ___ 4 ___ 5 ___ 5 ___ T ___ 5

A4-2
(Copy 2)

Melodic interval identification: Major thirds, perfect fourths and fifths, tritones

Shield the answer. Listen to the interval and write 3, 4, 5, or T in the blank; then uncover the answer and compare your response. Circle incorrect responses. Goal: No more than twelve errors.

1 ___ 4 ___ 5 ___ T ___ 4 ___ 3 ___ 4 ___ 5 ___ 4
2 ___ 4 ___ 4 ___ 4 ___ 5 ___ 4 ___ 5 ___ 4 ___ 5
3 ___ 4 ___ 5 ___ 3 ___ 4 ___ T ___ 5 ___ 4 ___ 5
4 ___ 4 ___ 4 ___ 4 ___ 5 ___ 4 ___ 5 ___ 4 ___ 5
5 ___ 5 ___ 4 ___ 5 ___ 4 ___ 4 ___ 5 ___ 5 ___ 4
6 ___ 5 ___ 4 ___ 4 ___ 5 ___ 5 ___ 4 ___ 5 ___ 5
7 ___ 5 ___ 3 ___ 4 ___ T ___ 5 ___ 5 ___ T ___ 4
8 ___ 3 ___ 4 ___ 5 ___ T ___ 5 ___ 4 ___ 3 ___ 4
9 ___ 4 ___ 4 ___ 5 ___ 4 ___ T ___ 5 ___ 4 ___ T
10 ___ 5 ___ 4 ___ T ___ 5 ___ 5 ___ 4 ___ T ___ 5
11 ___ 5 ___ 4 ___ 3 ___ 4 ___ T ___ 4 ___ T ___ 4
12 ___ 5 ___ 5 ___ T ___ 4 ___ 5 ___ 5 ___ T ___ 5

A4-2
(Copy 3)

Melodic interval identification: Major thirds, perfect fourths and fifths, tritones

Shield the answer. Listen to the interval and write 3, 4, 5, or T in the blank; then uncover the answer and compare your response. Circle incorrect responses. Goal: No more than twelve errors.

1 ___ 4 ___ 5 ___ T ___ 4 ___ 3 ___ 4 ___ 5 ___ 4
2 ___ 4 ___ 4 ___ 4 ___ 5 ___ 4 ___ 5 ___ 4 ___ 5
3 ___ 4 ___ 5 ___ 3 ___ 4 ___ T ___ 5 ___ 4 ___ 5
4 ___ 4 ___ 4 ___ 4 ___ 5 ___ 4 ___ 5 ___ 4 ___ 5
5 ___ 5 ___ 4 ___ 5 ___ 4 ___ 4 ___ 5 ___ 5 ___ 4
6 ___ 5 ___ 4 ___ 4 ___ 5 ___ 5 ___ 4 ___ 5 ___ 5
7 ___ 5 ___ 3 ___ 4 ___ T ___ 5 ___ 5 ___ T ___ 4
8 ___ 3 ___ 4 ___ 5 ___ T ___ 5 ___ 4 ___ 3 ___ 4
9 ___ 4 ___ 4 ___ 5 ___ 4 ___ T ___ 5 ___ 4 ___ T
10 ___ 5 ___ 4 ___ T ___ 5 ___ 5 ___ 4 ___ T ___ 5
11 ___ 5 ___ 4 ___ 3 ___ 4 ___ T ___ 4 ___ T ___ 4
12 ___ 5 ___ 5 ___ T ___ 4 ___ 5 ___ 5 ___ T ___ 5

A4-2
(Copy 4)

Melodic interval identification: Major thirds, perfect fourths and fifths, tritones

Shield the answer. Listen to the interval and write 3, 4, 5, or T in the blank; then uncover the answer and compare your response. Circle incorrect responses. Goal: No more than twelve errors.

1 ___ 4 ___ 5 ___ T ___ 4 ___ 3 ___ 4 ___ 5 ___ 4
2 ___ 4 ___ 4 ___ 4 ___ 5 ___ 4 ___ 5 ___ 4 ___ 5
3 ___ 4 ___ 5 ___ 3 ___ 4 ___ T ___ 5 ___ 4 ___ 5
4 ___ 4 ___ 4 ___ 4 ___ 5 ___ 4 ___ 5 ___ 4 ___ 5
5 ___ 5 ___ 4 ___ 5 ___ 4 ___ 4 ___ 5 ___ 5 ___ 4
6 ___ 5 ___ 4 ___ 4 ___ 5 ___ 5 ___ 4 ___ 5 ___ 5
7 ___ 5 ___ 3 ___ 4 ___ T ___ 5 ___ 5 ___ T ___ 4
8 ___ 3 ___ 4 ___ 5 ___ T ___ 5 ___ 4 ___ 3 ___ 4
9 ___ 4 ___ 4 ___ 5 ___ 4 ___ T ___ 5 ___ 4 ___ T
10 ___ 5 ___ 4 ___ T ___ 5 ___ 5 ___ 4 ___ T ___ 5
11 ___ 5 ___ 4 ___ 3 ___ 4 ___ T ___ 4 ___ T ___ 4
12 ___ 5 ___ 5 ___ T ___ 4 ___ 5 ___ 5 ___ T ___ 5

A4-2

(Copy 5)

Melodic interval identification: Major thirds, perfect fourths and fifths, tritones

Shield the answer. Listen to the interval and write 3, 4, 5, or T in the blank; then uncover the answer and compare your response. Circle incorrect responses. Goal: No more than twelve errors.

1 ___ 4 ___ 5 ___ T ___ 4 ___ 3 ___ 4 ___ 5 ___ 4

2 ___ 4 ___ 4 ___ 4 ___ 5 ___ 4 ___ 5 ___ 4 ___ 5

3 ___ 4 ___ 5 ___ 3 ___ 4 ___ T ___ 5 ___ 4 ___ 5

4 ___ 4 ___ 4 ___ 4 ___ 5 ___ 4 ___ 5 ___ 4 ___ 5

5 ___ 5 ___ 4 ___ 5 ___ 4 ___ 4 ___ 5 ___ 5 ___ 4

6 ___ 5 ___ 4 ___ 4 ___ 5 ___ 5 ___ 4 ___ 5 ___ 5

7 ___ 5 ___ 3 ___ 4 ___ T ___ 5 ___ 5 ___ T ___ 4

8 ___ 3 ___ 4 ___ 5 ___ T ___ 5 ___ 4 ___ 3 ___ 4

9 ___ 4 ___ 4 ___ 5 ___ 4 ___ T ___ 5 ___ 4 ___ T

10 ___ 5 ___ 4 ___ T ___ 5 ___ 5 ___ 4 ___ T ___ 5

11 ___ 5 ___ 4 ___ 3 ___ 4 ___ T ___ 4 ___ T ___ 4

12 ___ 5 ___ 5 ___ T ___ 4 ___ 5 ___ 5 ___ T ___ 5

67

A4-3
(Copy 1)

Melodic interval identification: Perfect fifths, major and minor sixths

Shield the answer. Listen to the interval and write 5, 6, or −6 in the blank; then uncover the answer and compare your response. Circle incorrect responses. Goal: No more than twelve errors.

1 —— 6 —— −6 —— 5 —— 6 —— −6 —— 6 —— 5 —— −6
2 —— 6 —— 5 —— −6 —— 6 —— 6 —— 5 —— −6 —— 6
3 —— −6 —— 5 —— 6 —— −6 —— 5 —— 6 —— 5 —— −6
4 —— −6 —— 6 —— 6 —— −6 —— 6 —— −6 —— 6 —— −6
5 —— 6 —— −6 —— 6 —— 6 —— 6 —— −6 —— −6 —— 6
6 —— 6 —— 5 —— −6 —— 6 —— 6 —— 5 —— −6 —— −6
7 —— 6 —— −6 —— 5 —— 6 —— 5 —— 6 —— 5 —— −6
8 —— 5 —— −6 —— 5 —— 6 —— 6 —— −6 —— 5 —— −6
9 —— 6 —— 5 —— −6 —— 5 —— −6 —— 5 —— 6 —— 6
10 —— 6 —— −6 —— 6 —— 5 —— −6 —— 6 —— 6 —— −6
11 —— 6 —— −6 —— 5 —— 5 —— 6 —— −6 —— 6 —— 5
12 —— 5 —— 6 —— −6 —— 5 —— 6 —— −6 —— 6 —— 5

A4-3
(Copy 2)

Melodic interval identification: Perfect fifths, major and minor sixths

Shield the answer. Listen to the interval and write 5, 6, or −6 in the blank; then uncover the answer and compare your response. Circle incorrect responses. Goal: No more than twelve errors.

1 —— 6 —— −6 —— 5 —— 6 —— −6 —— 6 —— 5 —— −6
2 —— 6 —— 5 —— −6 —— 6 —— 6 —— 5 —— −6 —— 6
3 —— −6 —— 5 —— 6 —— −6 —— 5 —— 6 —— 5 —— −6
4 —— −6 —— 6 —— 6 —— −6 —— 6 —— −6 —— 6 —— −6
5 —— 6 —— −6 —— 6 —— 6 —— 6 —— −6 —— −6 —— 6
6 —— 6 —— 5 —— −6 —— 6 —— 6 —— 5 —— −6 —— −6
7 —— 6 —— −6 —— 5 —— 6 —— 5 —— 6 —— 5 —— −6
8 —— 5 —— −6 —— 5 —— 6 —— 6 —— −6 —— 5 —— −6
9 —— 6 —— 5 —— −6 —— 5 —— −6 —— 5 —— 6 —— 6
10 —— 6 —— −6 —— 6 —— 5 —— −6 —— 6 —— 6 —— −6
11 —— 6 —— −6 —— 5 —— 5 —— 6 —— −6 —— 6 —— 5
12 —— 5 —— 6 —— −6 —— 5 —— 6 —— −6 —— 6 —— 5

A4-3
(Copy 3)

Melodic interval identification: Perfect fifths, major and minor sixths

Shield the answer. Listen to the interval and write 5, 6, or −6 in the blank; then uncover the answer and compare your response. Circle incorrect responses. Goal: No more than twelve errors.

1. ___ 6 ___ −6 ___ 5 ___ 6 ___ −6 ___ 6 ___ 5 ___ −6
2. ___ 6 ___ 5 ___ −6 ___ 6 ___ 6 ___ 5 ___ −6 ___ 6
3. ___ −6 ___ 5 ___ 6 ___ −6 ___ 5 ___ 6 ___ 5 ___ −6
4. ___ −6 ___ 6 ___ 6 ___ −6 ___ 6 ___ −6 ___ 6 ___ −6
5. ___ 6 ___ −6 ___ 6 ___ 6 ___ 6 ___ −6 ___ −6 ___ 6
6. ___ 6 ___ 5 ___ −6 ___ 6 ___ 6 ___ 5 ___ −6 ___ −6
7. ___ 6 ___ −6 ___ 5 ___ 6 ___ 5 ___ 6 ___ 5 ___ −6
8. ___ 5 ___ −6 ___ 5 ___ 6 ___ 6 ___ −6 ___ 5 ___ −6
9. ___ 6 ___ 5 ___ −6 ___ 5 ___ −6 ___ 5 ___ 6 ___ 6
10. ___ 6 ___ −6 ___ 6 ___ 5 ___ −6 ___ 6 ___ 6 ___ −6
11. ___ 6 ___ −6 ___ 5 ___ 5 ___ 6 ___ −6 ___ 6 ___ 5
12. ___ 5 ___ 6 ___ −6 ___ 5 ___ 6 ___ −6 ___ 6 ___ 5

A4-3
(Copy 4)

Melodic interval identification: Perfect fifths, major and minor sixths.

Shield the answer. Listen to the interval and write 5, 6, or −6 in the blank; then uncover the answer and compare your response. Circle incorrect responses. Goal: No more than twelve errors.

1. ___ 6 ___ −6 ___ 5 ___ 6 ___ −6 ___ 6 ___ 5 ___ −6
2. ___ 6 ___ 5 ___ −6 ___ 6 ___ 6 ___ 5 ___ −6 ___ 6
3. ___ −6 ___ 5 ___ 6 ___ −6 ___ 5 ___ 6 ___ 5 ___ −6
4. ___ −6 ___ 6 ___ 6 ___ −6 ___ 6 ___ −6 ___ 6 ___ −6
5. ___ 6 ___ −6 ___ 6 ___ 6 ___ 6 ___ −6 ___ −6 ___ 6
6. ___ 6 ___ 5 ___ −6 ___ 6 ___ 6 ___ 5 ___ −6 ___ −6
7. ___ 6 ___ −6 ___ 5 ___ 6 ___ 5 ___ 6 ___ 5 ___ −6
8. ___ 5 ___ −6 ___ 5 ___ 6 ___ 6 ___ −6 ___ 5 ___ −6
9. ___ 6 ___ 5 ___ −6 ___ 5 ___ −6 ___ 5 ___ 6 ___ 6
10. ___ 6 ___ −6 ___ 6 ___ 5 ___ −6 ___ 6 ___ 6 ___ −6
11. ___ 6 ___ −6 ___ 5 ___ 5 ___ 6 ___ −6 ___ 6 ___ 5
12. ___ 5 ___ 6 ___ −6 ___ 5 ___ 6 ___ −6 ___ 6 ___ 5

A4-3

(Copy 5)

Melodic interval identification: Perfect fifths, major and minor sixths

Shield the answer. Listen to the interval and write 5, 6, or −6 in the blank; then uncover the answer and compare your response. Circle incorrect responses. Goal: No more than twelve errors.

1	___	6	___	−6	___	5	___	6	___	−6	___	6	___	5	___	−6
2	___	6	___	5	___	−6	___	6	___	6	___	5	___	−6	___	6
3	___	−6	___	5	___	6	___	−6	___	5	___	6	___	5	___	−6
4	___	−6	___	6	___	6	___	−6	___	6	___	−6	___	6	___	−6
5	___	6	___	−6	___	6	___	6	___	6	___	−6	___	−6	___	6
6	___	6	___	5	___	−6	___	6	___	6	___	5	___	−6	___	−6
7	___	6	___	−6	___	5	___	6	___	5	___	6	___	5	___	−6
8	___	5	___	−6	___	5	___	6	___	6	___	−6	___	5	___	−6
9	___	6	___	5	___	−6	___	5	___	−6	___	5	___	6	___	6
10	___	6	___	−6	___	6	___	5	___	−6	___	6	___	6	___	−6
11	___	6	___	−6	___	5	___	5	___	6	___	−6	___	6	___	5
12	___	5	___	6	___	−6	___	5	___	6	___	−6	___	6	___	5

A4-4
(Copy 1)

Melodic interval identification: Major sixths; major and minor sevenths, perfect octaves

Shield the answer. Listen to the interval and write 6, 7, −7, or 8 in the blank; then uncover the answer and compare your response. Circle incorrect responses. Goal: No more than twelve errors.

1 ___ 8 ___ 7 ___ −7 ___ 6 ___ 8 ___ −7 ___ 7 ___ 8
2 ___ 8 ___ 7 ___ −7 ___ 8 ___ 7 ___ 8 ___ −7 ___ 7
3 ___ 7 ___ −7 ___ 8 ___ 7 ___ −7 ___ −7 ___ 7 ___ 6
4 ___ −7 ___ 7 ___ 7 ___ −7 ___ 8 ___ −7 ___ 7 ___ 7
5 ___ −7 ___ 7 ___ 8 ___ −7 ___ 7 ___ 7 ___ −7 ___ 6
6 ___ 8 ___ −7 ___ 8 ___ 7 ___ 8 ___ −7 ___ 8 ___ 7
7 ___ −7 ___ 8 ___ 7 ___ 6 ___ 7 ___ −7 ___ 8 ___ 7
8 ___ 8 ___ −7 ___ 8 ___ −7 ___ 6 ___ 6 ___ −7 ___ 7
9 ___ −7 ___ 7 ___ −7 ___ 6 ___ 7 ___ −7 ___ 7 ___ 8
10 ___ 6 ___ −7 ___ 8 ___ 7 ___ 7 ___ 7 ___ −7 ___ 8
11 ___ 8 ___ −7 ___ 6 ___ −7 ___ 8 ___ 6 ___ −7 ___ 7
12 ___ 8 ___ −7 ___ 8 ___ 7 ___ 7 ___ −7 ___ 6 ___ 8

A4-4
(Copy 2)

Melodic interval identification: Major sixths, major and minor sevenths, perfect octaves

Shield the answer. Listen to the interval and write 6, 7, −7, or 8 in the blank; then uncover the answer and compare your response. Circle incorrect responses. Goal: No more than twelve errors.

1 ___ 8 ___ 7 ___ −7 ___ 6 ___ 8 ___ −7 ___ 7 ___ 8
2 ___ 8 ___ 7 ___ −7 ___ 8 ___ 7 ___ 8 ___ −7 ___ 7
3 ___ 7 ___ −7 ___ 8 ___ 7 ___ −7 ___ −7 ___ 7 ___ 6
4 ___ −7 ___ 7 ___ 7 ___ −7 ___ 8 ___ −7 ___ 7 ___ 7
5 ___ −7 ___ 7 ___ 8 ___ −7 ___ 7 ___ 7 ___ −7 ___ 6
6 ___ 8 ___ −7 ___ 8 ___ 7 ___ 8 ___ −7 ___ 8 ___ 7
7 ___ −7 ___ 8 ___ 7 ___ 6 ___ 7 ___ −7 ___ 8 ___ 7
8 ___ 8 ___ −7 ___ 8 ___ −7 ___ 6 ___ 6 ___ −7 ___ 7
9 ___ −7 ___ 7 ___ −7 ___ 6 ___ 7 ___ −7 ___ 7 ___ 8
10 ___ 6 ___ −7 ___ 8 ___ 7 ___ 7 ___ 7 ___ −7 ___ 8
11 ___ 8 ___ −7 ___ 6 ___ −7 ___ 8 ___ 6 ___ −7 ___ 7
12 ___ 8 ___ −7 ___ 8 ___ 7 ___ 7 ___ −7 ___ 6 ___ 8

A4-4
(Copy 3)

Melodic interval identification: Major sixths, major and minor sevenths, perfect octaves

Shield the answer. Listen to the interval and write 6, 7, −7, or 8 in the blank; then uncover the answer and compare your response. Circle incorrect responses. Goal: No more than twelve errors.

1	___ 8	___ 7	___ −7	___ 6	___ 8	___ −7	___ 7	___ 8
2	___ 8	___ 7	___ −7	___ 8	___ 7	___ 8	___ −7	___ 7
3	___ 7	___ −7	___ 8	___ 7	___ −7	___ −7	___ 7	___ 6
4	___ −7	___ 7	___ 7	___ −7	___ 8	___ −7	___ 7	___ 7
5	___ −7	___ 7	___ 8	___ −7	___ 7	___ 7	___ −7	___ 6
6	___ 8	___ −7	___ 8	___ 7	___ 8	___ −7	___ 8	___ 7
7	___ −7	___ 8	___ 7	___ 6	___ 7	___ −7	___ 8	___ 7
8	___ 8	___ −7	___ 8	___ −7	___ 6	___ 6	___ −7	___ 7
9	___ −7	___ 7	___ −7	___ 6	___ 7	___ −7	___ 7	___ 8
10	___ 6	___ −7	___ 8	___ 7	___ 7	___ 7	___ −7	___ 8
11	___ 8	___ −7	___ 6	___ −7	___ 8	___ 6	___ −7	___ 7
12	___ 8	___ −7	___ 8	___ 7	___ 7	___ −7	___ 6	___ 8

A4-4
(Copy 4)

Melodic interval identification: Major sixths, major and minor sevenths, perfect octaves

Shield the answer. Listen to the interval and write 6, 7, −7, or 8 in the blank; then uncover the answer and compare your response. Circle incorrect responses. Goal: No more than twelve errors.

1	___ 8	___ 7	___ −7	___ 6	___ 8	___ −7	___ 7	___ 8
2	___ 8	___ 7	___ −7	___ 8	___ 7	___ 8	___ −7	___ 7
3	___ 7	___ −7	___ 8	___ 7	___ −7	___ −7	___ 7	___ 6
4	___ −7	___ 7	___ 7	___ −7	___ 8	___ −7	___ 7	___ 7
5	___ −7	___ 7	___ 8	___ −7	___ 7	___ 7	___ −7	___ 6
6	___ 8	___ −7	___ 8	___ 7	___ 8	___ −7	___ 8	___ 7
7	___ −7	___ 8	___ 7	___ 6	___ 7	___ −7	___ 8	___ 7
8	___ 8	___ −7	___ 8	___ −7	___ 6	___ 6	___ −7	___ 7
9	___ −7	___ 7	___ −7	___ 6	___ 7	___ −7	___ 7	___ 8
10	___ 6	___ −7	___ 8	___ 7	___ 7	___ 7	___ −7	___ 8
11	___ 8	___ −7	___ 6	___ −7	___ 8	___ 6	___ −7	___ 7
12	___ 8	___ −7	___ 8	___ 7	___ 7	___ −7	___ 6	___ 8

A4-4

(Copy 5)

Melodic interval identification: Major sixths, major and minor sevenths, perfect octaves

Shield the answer. Listen to the interval and write 6, 7, −7, or 8 in the blank; then uncover the answer and compare your response. Circle incorrect responses. Goal: No more than twelve errors.

1 ___ 8 ___ 7 ___ −7 ___ 6 ___ 8 ___ −7 ___ 7 ___ 8

2 ___ 8 ___ 7 ___ −7 ___ 8 ___ 7 ___ 8 ___ −7 ___ 7

3 ___ 7 ___ −7 ___ 8 ___ 7 ___ −7 ___ −7 ___ 7 ___ 6

4 ___ −7 ___ 7 ___ 7 ___ −7 ___ 8 ___ −7 ___ 7 ___ 7

5 ___ −7 ___ 7 ___ 8 ___ −7 ___ 7 ___ 7 ___ −7 ___ 6

6 ___ 8 ___ −7 ___ 8 ___ 7 ___ 8 ___ −7 ___ 8 ___ 7

7 ___ −7 ___ 8 ___ 7 ___ 6 ___ 7 ___ −7 ___ 8 ___ 7

8 ___ 8 ___ −7 ___ 8 ___ −7 ___ 6 ___ 6 ___ −7 ___ 7

9 ___ −7 ___ 7 ___ −7 ___ 6 ___ 7 ___ −7 ___ 7 ___ 8

10 ___ 6 ___ −7 ___ 8 ___ 7 ___ 7 ___ 7 ___ −7 ___ 8

11 ___ 8 ___ −7 ___ 6 ___ −7 ___ 8 ___ 6 ___ −7 ___ 7

12 ___ 8 ___ −7 ___ 8 ___ 7 ___ 7 ___ −7 ___ 6 ___ 8

A4-5
(Copy 1)

Melodic interval identification: All intervals previously studied

Shield the answer. Listen to the interval and write the symbol in the blank; then uncover the answer and compare your responses. Circle incorrect responses. Goal: No more than twelve errors.

1 ___ 8 ___ 5 ___ 3 ___ 4 ___ 2 ___ 5 ___ 4 ___ 8
2 ___ 5 ___ 3 ___ 2 ___ T ___ 5 ___ 6 ___ 7 ___ 8
3 ___ 8 ___ 5 ___ 3 ___ 4 ___ 6 ___ 5 ___ 7 ___ 2
4 ___ 8 ___ 3 ___ 4 ___ 5 ___ T ___ 4 ___ 7 ___ 8
5 ___ 2 ___ –2 ___ 3 ___ –3 ___ 5 ___ 6 ___ –6 ___ 4
6 ___ 7 ___ –7 ___ 6 ___ –6 ___ 3 ___ –3 ___ 6 ___ –6
7 ___ –7 ___ 7 ___ 6 ___ 4 ___ –6 ___ 3 ___ 5 ___ –3
8 ___ –2 ___ 5 ___ –7 ___ –3 ___ –6 ___ 7 ___ 4 ___ T
9 ___ 5 ___ T ___ 4 ___ 2 ___ 6 ___ –3 ___ 7 ___ 4
10 ___ –7 ___ 3 ___ 6 ___ –3 ___ 4 ___ 7 ___ 5 ___ 8
11 ___ 6 ___ 5 ___ 6 ___ 4 ___ T ___ 5 ___ –3 ___ 4
12 ___ 3 ___ –6 ___ 4 ___ 3 ___ 5 ___ –2 ___ –7 ___ 5

A4-5
(Copy 2)

Melodic interval identification: All intervals previously studied

Shield the answer. Listen to the interval and write the symbol in the blank; then uncover the answer and compare your response. Circle incorrect responses. Goal: No more than twelve errors.

1 ___ 8 ___ 5 ___ 3 ___ 4 ___ 2 ___ 5 ___ 4 ___ 8
2 ___ 5 ___ 3 ___ 2 ___ T ___ 5 ___ 6 ___ 7 ___ 8
3 ___ 8 ___ 5 ___ 3 ___ 4 ___ 6 ___ 5 ___ 7 ___ 2
4 ___ 8 ___ 3 ___ 4 ___ 5 ___ T ___ 4 ___ 7 ___ 8
5 ___ 2 ___ –2 ___ 3 ___ –3 ___ 5 ___ 6 ___ –6 ___ 4
6 ___ 7 ___ –7 ___ 6 ___ –6 ___ 3 ___ –3 ___ 6 ___ –6
7 ___ –7 ___ 7 ___ 6 ___ 4 ___ –6 ___ 3 ___ 5 ___ –3
8 ___ –2 ___ 5 ___ –7 ___ –3 ___ –6 ___ 7 ___ 4 ___ T
9 ___ 5 ___ T ___ 4 ___ 2 ___ 6 ___ –3 ___ 7 ___ 4
10 ___ –7 ___ 3 ___ 6 ___ –3 ___ 4 ___ 7 ___ 5 ___ 8
11 ___ 6 ___ 5 ___ 6 ___ 4 ___ T ___ 5 ___ –3 ___ 4
12 ___ 3 ___ –6 ___ 4 ___ 3 ___ 5 ___ –2 ___ –7 ___ 5

A4-5
(Copy 3)

Melodic interval identification: All intervals previously studied

Shield the answer. Listen to the interval and write the symbol in the blank; then uncover the answer and compare your response. Circle incorrect responses. Goal: No more than twelve errors.

1	___ 8	___ 5	___ 3	___ 4	___ 2	___ 5	___ 4	___ 8
2	___ 5	___ 3	___ 2	___ T	___ 5	___ 6	___ 7	___ 8
3	___ 8	___ 5	___ 3	___ 4	___ 6	___ 5	___ 7	___ 2
4	___ 8	___ 3	___ 4	___ 5	___ T	___ 4	___ 7	___ 8
5	___ 2	___ -2	___ 3	___ -3	___ 5	___ 6	___ -6	___ 4
6	___ 7	___ -7	___ 6	___ -6	___ 3	___ -3	___ 6	___ -6
7	___ -7	___ 7	___ 6	___ 4	___ -6	___ 3	___ 5	___ -3
8	___ -2	___ 5	___ -7	___ -3	___ -6	___ 7	___ 4	___ T
9	___ 5	___ T	___ 4	___ 2	___ 6	___ -3	___ 7	___ 4
10	___ -7	___ 3	___ 6	___ -3	___ 4	___ 7	___ 5	___ 8
11	___ 6	___ 5	___ 6	___ 4	___ T	___ 5	___ -3	___ 4
12	___ 3	___ -6	___ 4	___ 3	___ 5	___ -2	___ -7	___ 5

A4-5
(Copy 4)

Melodic interval identification: All intervals previously studied

Shield the answer. Listen to the interval and write the symbol in the blank; then uncover the answer and compare your response. Circle incorrect responses. Goal: No more than twelve errors.

1	___ 8	___ 5	___ 3	___ 4	___ 2	___ 5	___ 4	___ 8
2	___ 5	___ 3	___ 2	___ T	___ 5	___ 6	___ 7	___ 8
3	___ 8	___ 5	___ 3	___ 4	___ 6	___ 5	___ 7	___ 2
4	___ 8	___ 3	___ 4	___ 5	___ T	___ 4	___ 7	___ 8
5	___ 2	___ -2	___ 3	___ -3	___ 5	___ 6	___ -6	___ 4
6	___ 7	___ -7	___ 6	___ -6	___ 3	___ -3	___ 6	___ -6
7	___ -7	___ 7	___ 6	___ 4	___ -6	___ 3	___ 5	___ -3
8	___ -2	___ 5	___ -7	___ -3	___ -6	___ 7	___ 4	___ T
9	___ 5	___ T	___ 4	___ 2	___ 6	___ -3	___ 7	___ 4
10	___ -7	___ 3	___ 6	___ -3	___ 4	___ 7	___ 5	___ 8
11	___ 6	___ 5	___ 6	___ 4	___ T	___ 5	___ -3	___ 4
12	___ 3	___ -6	___ 4	___ 3	___ 5	___ -2	___ -7	___ 5

A4-5

(Copy 5)

Melodic interval identification: All intervals previously studied

Shield the answer. Listen to the interval and write the symbol in the blank; then uncover the answer and compare your response. Circle incorrect responses. Goal: No more than twelve errors.

1	___ 8	___ 5	___ 3	___ 4	___ 2	___ 5	___ 4	___ 8
2	___ 5	___ ·3	___ 2	___ T	___ 5	___ 6	___ 7	___ 8
3	___ 8	___ 5	___ 3	___ 4	___ 6	___ 5	___ 7	___ 2
4	___ 8	___ 3	___ 4	___ 5	___ T	___ 4	___ 7	___ 8
5	___ 2	___ -2	___ 3	___ -3	___ 5	___ 6	___ -6	___ 4
6	___ 7	___ -7	___ 6	___ -6	___ 3	___ -3	___ 6	___ -6
7	___ -7	___ 7	___ 6	___ 4	___ -6	___ 3	___ 5	___ -3
8	___ -2	___ 5	___ -7	___ -3	___ -6	___ 7	___ 4	___ T
9	___ 5	___ T	___ 4	___ 2	___ 6	___ -3	___ 7	___ 4
10	___ -7	___ 3	___ 6	___ -3	___ 4	___ 7	___ 5	___ 8
11	___ 6	___ 5	___ 6	___ 4	___ T	___ 5	___ -3	___ 4
12	___ 3	___ -6	___ 4	___ 3	___ 5	___ -2	___ -7	___ 5

A4-6
(Copy 1)

Melodic interval identification: All intervals previously studied

Shield the answer. Listen to the interval and write the symbol in the blank; then uncover the answer and compare your response. Circle incorrect responses. Goal: No more than twelve errors.

1 ___ 8 ___ 5 ___ 4 ___ −3 ___ 3 ___ 6 ___ 2 ___ 7

2 ___ 2 ___ 8 ___ 5 ___ 3 ___ 4 ___ 6 ___ 7 ___ 8

3 ___ 8 ___ 5 ___ T ___ 4 ___ −2 ___ 5 ___ 6 ___ −6

4 ___ −2 ___ 2 ___ 3 ___ 5 ___ 8 ___ 7 ___ 4 ___ 6

5 ___ 8 ___ 4 ___ 3 ___ 5 ___ T ___ 3 ___ 5 ___ 4

6 ___ 5 ___ 4 ___ 3 ___ 5 ___ T ___ 7 ___ 8 ___ 5

7 ___ 4 ___ 3 ___ 3 ___ 5 ___ 4 ___ −2 ___ 5 ___ −6

8 ___ 5 ___ 6 ___ 7 ___ 7 ___ −6 ___ 5 ___ −6 ___ 3

9 ___ −3 ___ −7 ___ 5 ___ 7 ___ 5 ___ 6 ___ −6 ___ 5

10 ___ 3 ___ 7 ___ 6 ___ 3 ___ −3 ___ −6 ___ 6 ___ 5

11 ___ 6 ___ 5 ___ T ___ −6 ___ 2 ___ 4 ___ −6 ___ −6

12 ___ 2 ___ 3 ___ T ___ 4 ___ 4 ___ −7 ___ 4 ___ −6

A4-6
(Copy 2)

Melodic interval identification: All intervals previously studied

Shield the answer. Listen to the interval and write the symbol in the blank; then uncover the answer and compare your response. Circle incorrect responses. Goal: No more than twelve errors.

1 ___ 8 ___ 5 ___ 4 ___ −3 ___ 3 ___ 6 ___ 2 ___ 7

2 ___ 2 ___ 8 ___ 5 ___ 3 ___ 4 ___ 6 ___ 7 ___ 8

3 ___ 8 ___ 5 ___ T ___ 4 ___ −2 ___ 5 ___ 6 ___ −6

4 ___ −2 ___ 2 ___ 3 ___ 5 ___ 8 ___ 7 ___ 4 ___ 6

5 ___ 8 ___ 4 ___ 3 ___ 5 ___ T ___ 3 ___ 5 ___ 4

6 ___ 5 ___ 4 ___ 3 ___ 5 ___ T ___ 7 ___ 8 ___ 5

7 ___ 4 ___ 3 ___ 3 ___ 5 ___ 4 ___ −2 ___ 5 ___ −6

8 ___ 5 ___ 6 ___ 7 ___ 7 ___ −6 ___ 5 ___ −6 ___ 3

9 ___ −3 ___ −7 ___ 5 ___ 7 ___ 5 ___ 6 ___ −6 ___ 5

10 ___ 3 ___ 7 ___ 6 ___ 3 ___ −3 ___ −6 ___ 6 ___ 5

11 ___ 6 ___ 5 ___ T ___ −6 ___ 2 ___ 4 ___ −6 ___ −6

12 ___ 2 ___ 3 ___ T ___ 4 ___ 4 ___ −7 ___ 4 ___ −6

A4-6
(Copy 3)

Melodic interval identification: All intervals previously studied

Shield the answer. Listen to the interval and write the symbol in the blank; then uncover the answer and compare your response. Circle incorrect responses. Goal: No more than twelve errors.

1	___ 8	___ 5	___ 4	___ −3	___ 3	___ 6	___ 2	___ 7
2	___ 2	___ 8	___ 5	___ 3	___ 4	___ 6	___ 7	___ 8
3	___ 8	___ 5	___ T	___ 4	___ −2	___ 5	___ 6	___ −6
4	___ −2	___ 2	___ 3	___ 5	___ 8	___ 7	___ 4	___ 6
5	___ 8	___ 4	___ 3	___ 5	___ T	___ 3	___ 5	___ 4
6	___ 5	___ 4	___ 3	___ 5	___ T	___ 7	___ 8	___ 5
7	___ 4	___ 3	___ 3	___ 5	___ 4	___ −2	___ 5	___ −6
8	___ 5	___ 6	___ 7	___ 7	___ −6	___ 5	___ −6	___ 3
9	___ −3	___ −7	___ 5	___ 7	___ 5	___ 6	___ −6	___ 5
10	___ 3	___ 7	___ 6	___ 3	___ −3	___ −6	___ 6	___ 5
11	___ 6	___ 5	___ T	___ −6	___ 2	___ 4	___ −6	___ −6
12	___ 2	___ 3	___ T	___ 4	___ 4	___ −7	___ 4	___ −6

A4-6
(Copy 4)

Melodic interval identification: All intervals previously studied

Shield the answer. Listen to the interval and write the symbol in the blank; then uncover the answer and compare your response. Circle incorrect responses. Goal: No more than twelve errors.

1	___ 8	___ 5	___ 4	___ −3	___ 3	___ 6	___ 2	___ 7
2	___ 2	___ 8	___ 5	___ 3	___ 4	___ 6	___ 7	___ 8
3	___ 8	___ 5	___ T	___ 4	___ −2	___ 5	___ 6	___ −6
4	___ −2	___ 2	___ 3	___ 5	___ 8	___ 7	___ 4	___ 6
5	___ 8	___ 4	___ 3	___ 5	___ T	___ 3	___ 5	___ 4
6	___ 5	___ 4	___ 3	___ 5	___ T	___ 7	___ 8	___ 5
7	___ 4	___ 3	___ 3	___ 5	___ 4	___ −2	___ 5	___ −6
8	___ 5	___ 6	___ 7	___ 7	___ −6	___ 5	___ −6	___ 3
9	___ −3	___ −7	___ 5	___ 7	___ 5	___ 6	___ −6	___ 5
10	___ 3	___ 7	___ 6	___ 3	___ −3	___ −6	___ 6	___ 5
11	___ 6	___ 5	___ T	___ −6	___ 2	___ 4	___ −6	___ −6
12	___ 2	___ 3	___ T	___ 4	___ 4	___ −7	___ 4	___ −7

A4-6
(Copy 5)

Melodic interval identification: All intervals previously studied

Shield the answer. Listen to the interval and write the symbol in the blank; then uncover the answer and compare your response. Circle incorrect responses. Goal: No more than twelve errors.

1 ___ 8 ___ 5 ___ 4 ___ −3 ___ 3 ___ 6 ___ 2 ___ 7

2 ___ 2 ___ 8 ___ 5 ___ 3 ___ 4 ___ 6 ___ 7 ___ 8

3 ___ 8 ___ 5 ___ T ___ 4 ___ −2 ___ 5 ___ 6 ___ −6

4 ___ −2 ___ 2 ___ 3 ___ 5 ___ 8 ___ 7 ___ 4 ___ 6

5 ___ 8 ___ 4 ___ 3 ___ 5 ___ T ___ 3 ___ 5 ___ 4

6 ___ 5 ___ 4 ___ 3 ___ 5 ___ T ___ 7 ___ 8 ___ 5

7 ___ 4 ___ 3 ___ 3 ___ 5 ___ 4 ___ −2 ___ 5 ___ −6

8 ___ 5 ___ 6 ___ 7 ___ 7 ___ −6 ___ 5 ___ −6 ___ 3

9 ___ −3 ___ −7 ___ 5 ___ 7 ___ 5 ___ 6 ___ −6 ___ 5

10 ___ 3 ___ 7 ___ 6 ___ 3 ___ −3 ___ −6 ___ 6 ___ 5

11 ___ 6 ___ 5 ___ T ___ −6 ___ 2 ___ 4 ___ −6 ___ −6

12 ___ 2 ___ 3 ___ T ___ 4 ___ 4 ___ −7 ___ 4 ___ −6

A4-7
(Copy 1)

Melodic interval identification: All intervals previously studied

Shield the answer. Listen to the interval and write the symbol in the blank; then check your response. Circle incorrect responses. Goal: No more than twelve errors. After your have done this lesson, take Test A4.

1	___ 5	___ 3	___ −3	___ 4	___ 5	___ 2	___ −2	___ 5
2	___ 6	___ −3	___ 5	___ −6	___ 5	___ 3	___ −3	___ 4
3	___ 4	___ 5	___ 6	___ 2	___ 8	___ 5	___ −6	___ 7
4	___ 8	___ 2	___ 7	___ 3	___ 4	___ T	___ 5	___ 4
5	___ 7	___ 3	___ −7	___ 5	___ −6	___ 7	___ 3	___ −3
6	___ 5	___ 6	___ 5	___ −6	___ 3	___ −2	___ 5	___ −6
7	___ 8	___ −7	___ 5	___ 6	___ −3	___ 3	___ 5	___ −6
8	___ 4	___ T	___ 7	___ 5	___ 6	___ −7	___ 5	___ T
9	___ 3	___ −3	___ 2	___ 5	___ −6	___ 7	___ 6	___ 4
10	___ 5	___ −6	___ 4	___ T	___ 4	___ 5	___ 6	___ 5
11	___ 2	___ −7	___ −6	___ 6	___ 4	___ T	___ −3	___ −3
12	___ T	___ 6	___ −6	___ −3	___ 7	___ −7	___ −3	___ −6

A4-7
(Copy 2)

Melodic interval identification: All intervals previously studied

Shield the answer. Listen to the interval and write the symbol in the blank; then check your response. Circle incorrect responses. Goal: No more than twelve errors. After you have done this lesson, take Test A4.

1	___ 5	___ 3	___ −3	___ 4	___ 5	___ 2	___ −2	___ 5
2	___ 6	___ −3	___ 5	___ −6	___ 5	___ 3	___ −3	___ 4
3	___ 4	___ 5	___ 6	___ 2	___ 8	___ 5	___ −6	___ 7
4	___ 8	___ 2	___ 7	___ 3	___ 4	___ T	___ 5	___ 4
5	___ 7	___ 3	___ −7	___ 5	___ −6	___ 7	___ 3	___ −3
6	___ 5	___ 6	___ 5	___ −6	___ 3	___ −2	___ 5	___ −6
7	___ 8	___ −7	___ 5	___ 6	___ −3	___ 3	___ 5	___ −6
8	___ 4	___ T	___ 7	___ 5	___ 6	___ −7	___ 5	___ T
9	___ 3	___ −3	___ 2	___ 5	___ −6	___ 7	___ 6	___ 4
10	___ 5	___ −6	___ 4	___ T	___ 4	___ 5	___ 6	___ 5
11	___ 2	___ −7	___ −6	___ 6	___ 4	___ T	___ −3	___ −3
12	___ T	___ 6	___ −6	___ −3	___ 7	___ −7	___ −3	___ −6

A4-7
(Copy 3)

Melodic interval identification: All intervals previously studied

Shield the answer. Listen to the interval and write the symbol in the blank; then check your response. Circle incorrect responses. Goal: No more than twelve errors. After you have done this lesson, take Test A4.

1 ___ 5 ___ 3 ___ −3 ___ 4 ___ 5 ___ 2 ___ −2 ___ 5

2 ___ 6 ___ −3 ___ 5 ___ −6 ___ 5 ___ 3 ___ −3 ___ 4

3 ___ 4 ___ 5 ___ 6 ___ 2 ___ 8 ___ 5 ___ −6 ___ 7

4 ___ 8 ___ 2 ___ 7 ___ 3 ___ 4 ___ T ___ 5 ___ 4

5 ___ 7 ___ 3 ___ −7 ___ 5 ___ −6 ___ 7 ___ 3 ___ −3

6 ___ 5 ___ 6 ___ 5 ___ −6 ___ 3 ___ −2 ___ 5 ___ −6

7 ___ 8 ___ −7 ___ 5 ___ 6 ___ −3 ___ 3 ___ 5 ___ −6

8 ___ 4 ___ T ___ 7 ___ 5 ___ 6 ___ −7 ___ 5 ___ T

9 ___ 3 ___ −3 ___ 2 ___ 5 ___ −6 ___ 7 ___ 6 ___ 4

10 ___ 5 ___ −6 ___ 4 ___ T ___ 4 ___ 5 ___ 6 ___ 5

11 ___ 2 ___ −7 ___ −6 ___ 6 ___ 4 ___ T ___ −3 ___ −3

12 ___ T ___ 6 ___ −6 ___ −3 ___ 7 ___ −7 ___ −3 ___ −6

A4-7
(Copy 4)

Melodic interval identification: All intervals previously studied

Shield the answer. Listen to the interval and write the symbol in the blank; then check your response. Circle incorrect responses. Goal: No more than twelve errors. After you have done this lesson, take Test A4.

1 ___ 5 ___ 3 ___ −3 ___ 4 ___ 5 ___ 2 ___ −2 ___ 5

2 ___ 6 ___ −3 ___ 5 ___ −6 ___ 5 ___ 3 ___ −3 ___ 4

3 ___ 4 ___ 5 ___ 6 ___ 2 ___ 8 ___ 5 ___ −6 ___ 7

4 ___ 8 ___ 2 ___ 7 ___ 3 ___ 4 ___ T ___ 5 ___ 4

5 ___ 7 ___ 3 ___ −7 ___ 5 ___ −6 ___ 7 ___ 3 ___ −3

6 ___ 5 ___ 6 ___ 5 ___ −6 ___ 3 ___ −2 ___ 5 ___ −6

7 ___ 8 ___ −7 ___ 5 ___ 6 ___ −3 ___ 3 ___ 5 ___ −6

8 ___ 4 ___ T ___ 7 ___ 5 ___ 6 ___ −7 ___ 5 ___ T

9 ___ 3 ___ −3 ___ 2 ___ 5 ___ −6 ___ 7 ___ 6 ___ 4

10 ___ 5 ___ −6 ___ 4 ___ T ___ 4 ___ 5 ___ 6 ___ 5

11 ___ 2 ___ −7 ___ −6 ___ 6 ___ 4 ___ T ___ −3 ___ −3

12 ___ T ___ 6 ___ −6 ___ −3 ___ 7 ___ −7 ___ −3 ___ −6

A4-7

(Copy 5)

Melodic interval identification: All intervals previously studied

Shield the answer. Listen to the interval and write the symbol in the blank; then check your response. Circle incorrect responses. Goal: No more than twelve errors. After you have done this lesson, take Test A4.

1	___	5	___	3	___	−3	___	4	___	5	___	2	___	−2	___	5
2	___	6	___	−3	___	5	___	−6	___	5	___	3	___	−3	___	4
3	___	4	___	5	___	6	___	2	___	8	___	5	___	−6	___	7
4	___	8	___	2	___	7	___	3	___	4	___	T	___	5	___	4
5	___	7	___	3	___	−7	___	5	___	−6	___	7	___	3	___	−3
6	___	5	___	6	___	5	___	−6	___	3	___	−2	___	5	___	−6
7	___	8	___	−7	___	5	___	6	___	−3	___	3	___	5	___	−6
8	___	4	___	T	___	7	___	5	___	6	___	−7	___	5	___	T
9	___	3	___	−3	___	2	___	5	___	−6	___	7	___	6	___	4
10	___	5	___	−6	___	4	___	T	___	4	___	5	___	6	___	5
11	___	2	___	−7	___	−6	___	6	___	4	___	T	___	−3	___	−3
12	___	T	___	6	___	−6	___	−3	___	7	___	−7	___	−3	___	−6

Harmonic Interval Discrimination SERIES A5

In this series the two tones of the interval are sounded at the same time. Such intervals are called harmonic intervals.

As in the interval discrimination lessons you did in Series A1, your task here is to discriminate, from all the intervals heard, those of a particular size. The procedure is the same as in the earlier series. You will hear an interval followed by a very brief pause during which you are to decide whether the interval you have just heard is the one you have been asked to discriminate. If it is, make a tally mark. You will hear an electronic signal whenever the interval is the one you are to discriminate. You are correct if you make a mark and then hear the signal, or if you do not make a mark and do not hear the signal. Start a new row of tally marks when you make a mistake. When you have made fifteen correct tally marks in a row, go on to the next lesson.

The discrimination interval for each lesson in this series is as follows:

A5–1	minor second
A5–2	major second
A5–3	minor third
A5–4	major third
A5–5	perfect fourth
A5–6	tritone
A5–7	perfect fifth
A5–8	minor sixth
A5–9	major sixth
A5–10	minor seventh
A5–11	major seventh

The lessons may be done in any order. It is convenient to do them in the above order, but if the tape you need is in use, do another lesson.

There is no test for this series. While your achievement in harmonic interval discrimination is not tested, this skill will help you in the series that follow, for which there are tests.

Harmonic Interval Dictation   SERIES A6

The purpose of this series is to develop your ability to write harmonic intervals that you hear. A printed worksheet and a tape recording are provided for each lesson. The frames on the worksheet are separated by bar lines. At the beginning of each frame, you will find a note that corresponds to the lower tone of the harmonic interval that you will hear. The complete interval is shown at the end of the frame.

To do each frame, start by shielding the interval at the end of the frame. When you have heard the interval, write the upper note of the interval above the given note. Then slide the shield to the right and compare your response with the printed answer. Circle the frame if your response is incorrect.

Your goal is to complete each lesson with no more than twelve errors. When you have done so, go on to the next lesson. If you have made more than twelve errors, repeat the lesson until you reach the goal or until you have done the lesson five times, at which point you should go on to the next lesson regardless of your score.

There is one test for this series, to be taken following lesson A6-7.

A6-1 Harmonic interval dictation: Major and minor seconds
(Copy 1)

Shield the answer. Listen to the interval and notate the upper tone above the given note; then uncover the answer and compare your response. Circle incorrect responses. Goal: No more than twelve errors.

A6-1
(Copy 2)

Harmonic interval dictation: Major and minor seconds

Shield the answer. Listen to the interval and notate the upper tone above the given note; then uncover the answer and compare your response. Circle incorrect responses. Goal: No more than twelve errors.

A6–1 Harmonic interval dictation: Major and minor seconds

(Copy 3)

Shield the answer. Listen to the interval and notate the upper tone above the given note; then uncover the answer and compare your response. Circle incorrect responses. Goal: No more than twelve errors.

A6-1
(Copy 4)

Harmonic interval dictation: Major and minor seconds

Shield the answer. Listen to the interval and notate the upper tone above the given note; then uncover the answer and compare your response. Circle incorrect responses. Goal: No more than twelve errors.

89

A6-1 Harmonic interval dictation: Major and minor seconds

(Copy 5)

Shield the answer. Listen to the interval and notate the upper tone above the given note; then uncover the answer and compare your response. Circle incorrect responses. Goal: No more than twelve errors.

A6-2
Harmonic interval dictation: Major and minor thirds

Shield the answer. Listen to the interval and notate the upper tone above the given note; then uncover the answer and compare your response. Circle incorrect responses. Goal: No more than twelve errors.

91

A6-2 Harmonic interval dictation: Major and minor thirds

(Copy 2)

Shield the answer. Listen to the interval and notate the upper tone above the given note; then uncover the answer and compare your response. Circle incorrect responses. Goal: No more than twelve errors.

A6-2 Harmonic interval dictation: Major and minor thirds

(Copy 3)

Shield the answer. Listen to the interval and notate the upper tone above the given note; then uncover the answer and compare your response. Circle incorrect responses. Goal: No more than twelve errors.

A6-2
Harmonic interval dictation: Major and minor thirds

Shield the answer. Listen to the interval and notate the upper tone above the given note; then uncover the answer and compare your response. Circle incorrect responses. Goal: No more than twelve errors.

A6-2

(Copy 5)

Harmonic interval dictation: Major and minor thirds

Shield the answer. Listen to the interval and notate the upper tone above the given note; then uncover the answer and compare your response. Circle incorrect responses. Goal: No more than twelve errors.

95

A6-3
(Copy 1)

Harmonic interval dictation: Perfect and augmented fourths, perfect and diminished fifths

Shield the answer. Listen to the interval and notate the upper tone above the given note; then uncover the answer and compare your response. Circle incorrect responses. Goal: No more than twelve errors.

A6-3
(Copy 2)

Harmonic interval dictation: Perfect and augmented fourths, perfect and diminished fifths

Shield the answer. Listen to the interval and notate the upper tone above the given note; then uncover the answer and compare your response. Circle incorrect responses. Goal: No more than twelve errors.

Harmonic interval dictation: Perfect and augmented fourths, perfect and diminished fifths

Shield the answer. Listen to the interval and notate the upper tone above the given note; then uncover the answer and compare your response. Circle incorrect responses. Goal: No more than twelve errors.

A6-3

Harmonic interval dictation: Perfect and augmented fourths, perfect and diminished fifths

Shield the answer. Listen to the interval and notate the upper tone above the given note; then uncover the answer and compare your response. Circle incorrect responses. Goal: No more than twelve errors.

99

A6-3

Harmonic interval dictation: Perfect and augmented fourths, perfect and diminished fifths

Shield the answer. Listen to the interval and notate the upper tone above the given note; then uncover the answer and compare your response. Circle incorrect responses. Goal: No more than twelve errors.

100

A6-4 Harmonic interval dictation: Major and minor sixths

(Copy 1)

Shield the answer. Listen to the interval and notate the upper tone above the given note; then uncover the answer and compare your response. Circle incorrect responses. Goal: No more than twelve errors.

Harmonic interval dictation: Major and minor sixths

Shield the answer. Listen to the interval and notate the upper tone above the given note; then uncover the answer and compare your response. Circle incorrect responses. Goal: No more than twelve errors.

A6-4

Harmonic interval dictation: Major and minor sixths

Shield the answer. Listen to the interval and notate the upper tone above the given note; then uncover the answer and compare your response. Circle incorrect responses. Goal: No more than twelve errors.

103

A6-4

Harmonic interval dictation: Major and minor sixths

Shield the answer. Listen to the interval and notate the upper tone above the given note; then uncover the answer and compare your response. Circle incorrect responses. Goal: No more than twelve errors.

A6-4 Harmonic interval dictation: Major and minor sixths

(Copy 5)

Shield the answer. Listen to the interval and notate the upper tone above the given note; then uncover the answer and compare your response. Circle incorrect responses. Goal: No more than twelve errors.

Harmonic interval dictation: Major and minor sevenths, perfect octaves

Shield the answer. Listen to the interval and notate the upper tone above the given note; then uncover the answer and compare your response. Circle incorrect responses. Goal: No more than twelve errors.

A6-5

(Copy 2)

Harmonic interval dictation: Major and minor sevenths, perfect octaves

Shield the answer. Listen to the interval and notate the upper tone above the given note; then uncover the answer and compare your response. Circle incorrect responses. Goal: No more than twelve errors.

A6-5 Harmonic interval dictation: Major and minor sevenths, perfect octaves
(Copy 3)

Shield the answer. Listen to the interval and notate the upper tone above the given note; then uncover the answer and compare your response. Circle incorrect responses. Goal: No more than twelve errors.

A6–5
(Copy 4)

Harmonic interval dictation: Major and minor sevenths, perfect octaves

Shield the answer. Listen to the interval and notate the upper tone above the given note; then uncover the answer and compare your response. Circle incorrect responses. Goal: No more than twelve errors.

A6-5

Harmonic interval dictation: Major and minor sevenths, perfect octaves

Shield the answer. Listen to the interval and notate the upper tone above the given note; then uncover the answer and compare your response. Circle incorrect responses. Goal: No more than twelve errors.

Harmonic interval dictation: All intervals previously studied

Shield the answer. Listen to the interval and notate the upper tone above the given note; then uncover the answer and compare your response. Circle incorrect responses. Goal: No more than twelve errors.

A6-6

Harmonic interval dictation: All intervals previously studied

Shield the answer. Listen to the interval and notate the upper tone above the given note; then uncover the answer and compare your response. Circle incorrect responses. Goal: No more than twelve errors.

112

A6-6 Harmonic interval dictation: All intervals previously studied

(Copy 3)

Shield the answer. Listen to the interval and notate the upper tone above the given note; then uncover the answer and compare your response. Circle incorrect responses. Goal: No more than twelve errors.

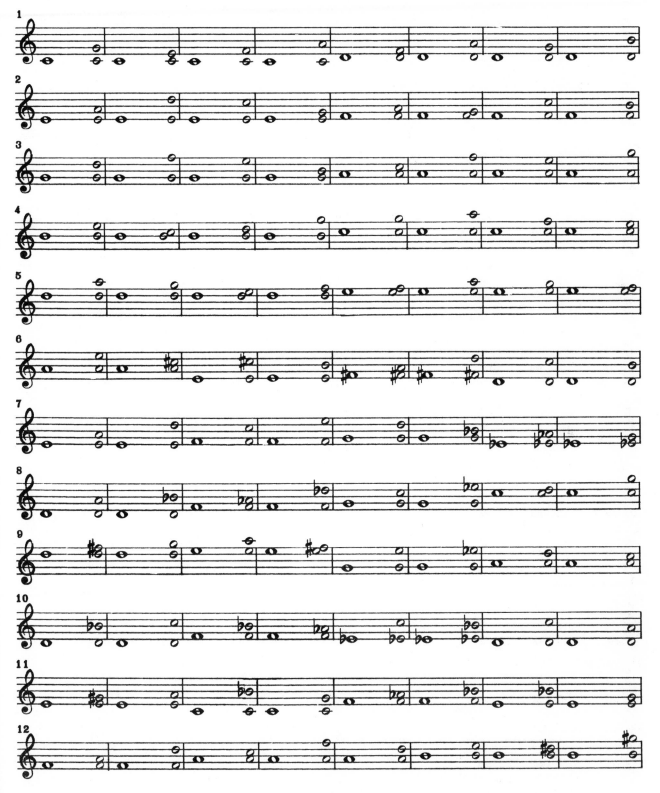

A6-6

Harmonic interval dictation: All intervals previously studied

Shield the answer. Listen to the interval and notate the upper tone above the given note; then uncover the answer and compare your response. Circle incorrect responses. Goal: No more than twelve errors.

A6-6

(Copy 5)

Harmonic interval dictation: All intervals previously studied

Shield the answer. Listen to the interval and notate the upper tone above the given note; then uncover the answer and compare your response. Circle incorrect responses. Goal: No more than twelve errors.

Harmonic interval dictation: All intervals previously studied

Shield the answer. Listen to the interval and notate the upper tone; then check your response. Circle incorrect responses. Goal: No more than twelve errors. After you have done this lesson, take Test A6.

A6-7
(Copy 2)

Harmonic interval dictation: All intervals previously studied

Shield the answer. Listen to the interval and notate the upper tone; then check your response. Circle
• incorrect responses. Goal: No more than twelve errors. After you have done this lesson, take Test A6.

A6-7

Harmonic interval dictation: All intervals previously studied

Shield the answer. Listen to the interval and notate the upper tone; then check your response. Circle incorrect responses. Goal: No more than twelve errors. After you have done this lesson, take Test A6.

A6-7
(Copy 4)

Harmonic interval dictation: All intervals previously studied

Shield the answer. Listen to the interval and notate the upper tone; then check your response. Circle incorrect responses. Goal: No more than twelve errors. After your have done this lesson, take Test A6.

Harmonic interval dictation: All intervals previously studied

Shield the answer. Listen to the interval and notate the upper tone; then check your response. Circle incorrect responses. Goal: No more than twelve errors. After you have done this lesson, take Test A6.

Harmonic Interval Identification   SERIES A7

The purpose of this series is to develop your ability to identify the size of harmonic intervals you hear. The same symbols used to identify melodic intervals in Series A4 will be used here. The procedure is the same as in the earlier series. You are to shield the answer while you listen to the interval and write the symbol for it in the blank. Then slide the shield to the right and compare your response with the printed answer. Circle the frame if your response is incorrect.

Your goal is to complete each lesson with no more than twelve errors. When you have done so, go on to the next lesson. If you have made more than twelve errors, repeat the lesson until you reach the goal or until you have done the lesson five times, at which point you should go on to the next lesson regardless of your score.

There is one test for this series, to be taken following lesson A7-8.

A7-1
(Copy 1)

Harmonic interval identification: Major and minor seconds

Shield the answer. Listen to the interval and write 2 or −2 in the blank; then uncover the answer and compare your response. Circle incorrect responses. Goal: No more than twelve errors.

1 ___ −2 ___ 2 ___ 2 ___ −2 ___ −2 ___ 2 ___ −2 ___ 2

2 ___ −2 ___ 2 ___ 2 ___ −2 ___ 2 ___ −2 ___ −2 ___ 2

3 ___ −2 ___ 2 ___ 2 ___ −2 ___ 2 ___ −2 ___ −2 ___ 2

4 ___ 2 ___ −2 ___ −2 ___ 2 ___ 2 ___ −2 ___ −2 ___ 2

5 ___ −2 ___ 2 ___ 2 ___ −2 ___ −2 ___ 2 ___ −2 ___ 2

6 ___ 2 ___ −2 ___ −2 ___ 2 ___ 2 ___ −2 ___ −2 ___ 2

7 ___ 2 ___ −2 ___ −2 ___ 2 ___ −2 ___ −2 ___ 2 ___ 2

8 ___ 2 ___ −2 ___ −2 ___ −2 ___ −2 ___ 2 ___ 2 ___ 2

9 ___ −2 ___ −2 ___ 2 ___ −2 ___ −2 ___ 2 ___ 2 ___ −2

10 ___ −2 ___ 2 ___ 2 ___ −2 ___ 2 ___ 2 ___ −2 ___ −2

11 ___ 2 ___ −2 ___ 2 ___ −2 ___ −2 ___ 2 ___ −2 ___ 2

12 ___ −2 ___ 2 ___ 2 ___ −2 ___ −2 ___ −2 ___ 2 ___ 2

A7-1
(Copy 2)

Harmonic interval identification: Major and minor seconds

Shield the answer. Listen to the interval and write 2 or −2 in the blank; then uncover the answer and compare your response. Circle incorrect responses. Goal: No more than twelve errors.

1 ___ −2 ___ 2 ___ 2 ___ −2 ___ −2 ___ 2 ___ −2 ___ 2

2 ___ −2 ___ 2 ___ 2 ___ −2 ___ 2 ___ −2 ___ −2 ___ 2

3 ___ −2 ___ 2 ___ 2 ___ −2 ___ 2 ___ −2 ___ −2 ___ 2

4 ___ 2 ___ −2 ___ −2 ___ 2 ___ 2 ___ −2 ___ −2 ___ 2

5 ___ −2 ___ 2 ___ 2 ___ −2 ___ −2 ___ 2 ___ −2 ___ 2

6 ___ 2 ___ −2 ___ −2 ___ 2 ___ 2 ___ −2 ___ −2 ___ 2

7 ___ 2 ___ −2 ___ −2 ___ 2 ___ −2 ___ −2 ___ 2 ___ 2

8 ___ 2 ___ −2 ___ −2 ___ −2 ___ −2 ___ 2 ___ 2 ___ 2

9 ___ −2 ___ −2 ___ 2 ___ −2 ___ −2 ___ 2 ___ 2 ___ −2

10 ___ −2 ___ 2 ___ 2 ___ −2 ___ 2 ___ 2 ___ −2 ___ −2

11 ___ 2 ___ −2 ___ 2 ___ −2 ___ −2 ___ 2 ___ −2 ___ 2

12 ___ −2 ___ 2 ___ 2 ___ −2 ___ −2 ___ −2 ___ 2 ___ 2

A7-1
(Copy 3)

Harmonic interval identification: Major and minor seconds

Shield the answer. Listen to the interval and write 2 or −2 in the blank; then uncover the answer and compare your response. Circle incorrect responses. Goal: No more than twelve errors.

1	___ −2	___ 2	___ 2	___ −2	___ −2	___ 2	___ −2	___ 2
2	___ −2	___ 2	___ 2	___ −2	___ 2	___ −2	___ −2	___ 2
3	___ −2	___ 2	___ 2	___ −2	___ 2	___ −2	___ −2	___ 2
4	___ 2	___ −2	___ −2	___ 2	___ 2	___ −2	___ −2	___ 2
5	___ −2	___ 2	___ 2	___ −2	___ −2	___ 2	___ −2	___ 2
6	___ 2	___ −2	___ −2	___ 2	___ 2	___ −2	___ −2	___ 2
7	___ 2	___ −2	___ −2	___ 2	___ −2	___ −2	___ 2	___ 2
8	___ 2	___ −2	___ −2	___ −2	___ −2	___ 2	___ 2	___ 2
9	___ −2	___ −2	___ 2	___ −2	___ −2	___ 2	___ 2	___ −2
10	___ −2	___ 2	___ 2	___ −2	___ 2	___ 2	___ −2	___ −2
11	___ 2	___ −2	___ 2	___ −2	___ −2	___ 2	___ −2	___ 2
12	___ −2	___ 2	___ 2	___ −2	___ −2	___ −2	___ 2	___ 2

A7-1
(Copy 4)

Harmonic interval identification: Major and minor seconds

Shield the answer. Listen to the interval and write 2 or −2 in the blank; then uncover the answer and compare your response. Circle incorrect responses. Goal: No more than twelve errors.

1	___ −2	___ 2	___ 2	___ −2	___ −2	___ 2	___ −2	___ 2
2	___ −2	___ 2	___ 2	___ −2	___ 2	___ −2	___ −2	___ 2
3	___ −2	___ 2	___ 2	___ −2	___ 2	___ −2	___ −2	___ 2
4	___ 2	___ −2	___ −2	___ 2	___ 2	___ −2	___ −2	___ 2
5	___ −2	___ 2	___ 2	___ −2	___ −2	___ 2	___ −2	___ 2
6	___ 2	___ −2	___ −2	___ 2	___ 2	___ −2	___ −2	___ 2
7	___ 2	___ −2	___ −2	___ 2	___ −2	___ −2	___ 2	___ 2
8	___ 2	___ −2	___ −2	___ −2	___ −2	___ 2	___ 2	___ 2
9	___ −2	___ −2	___ 2	___ −2	___ −2	___ 2	___ 2	___ −2
10	___ −2	___ 2	___ 2	___ −2	___ 2	___ 2	___ −2	___ −2
11	___ 2	___ −2	___ 2	___ −2	___ −2	___ 2	___ −2	___ 2
12	___ −2	___ 2	___ 2	___ −2	___ −2	___ −2	___ 2	___ 2

A7-1
(Copy 5)

Harmonic interval identification: Major and minor seconds

Shield the answer. Listen to the interval and write 2 or −2 in the blank; then uncover the answer and compare your response. Circle incorrect responses. Goal: No more than twelve errors.

1 ____ −2 ____ 2 ____ 2 ____ −2 ____ −2 ____ 2 ____ −2 ____ 2

2 ____ −2 ____ 2 ____ 2 ____ −2 ____ 2 ____ −2 ____ −2 ____ 2

3 ____ −2 ____ 2 ____ 2 ____ −2 ____ 2 ____ −2 ____ −2 ____ 2

4 ____ 2 ____ −2 ____ −2 ____ 2 ____ 2 ____ −2 ____ −2 ____ 2

5 ____ −2 ____ 2 ____ 2 ____ −2 ____ −2 ____ 2 ____ −2 ____ 2

6 ____ 2 ____ −2 ____ −2 ____ 2 ____ 2 ____ −2 ____ −2 ____ 2

7 ____ 2 ____ −2 ____ −2 ____ 2 ____ −2 ____ −2 ____ 2 ____ 2

8 ____ 2 ____ −2 ____ −2 ____ −2 ____ −2 ____ 2 ____ 2 ____ 2

9 ____ −2 ____ −2 ____ 2 ____ −2 ____ −2 ____ 2 ____ 2 ____ −2

10 ____ −2 ____ 2 ____ 2 ____ −2 ____ 2 ____ 2 ____ −2 ____ −2

11 ____ 2 ____ −2 ____ 2 ____ −2 ____ −2 ____ 2 ____ −2 ____ 2

12 ____ −2 ____ 2 ____ 2 ____ −2 ____ −2 ____ −2 ____ 2 ____ 2

A7-2
(Copy 1)

Harmonic interval identification: Major and minor thirds

Shield the answer. Listen to the interval and write 3 or −3 in the blank; then uncover the answer and compare your response. Circle incorrect responses. Goal: No more than twelve errors.

1 ____ 3 ____ −3 ____ 3 ____ −3 ____ −3 ____ 3 ____ −3 ____ 3

2 ____ 3 ____ −3 ____ −3 ____ 3 ____ 3 ____ −3 ____ −3 ____ 3

3 ____ 3 ____ −3 ____ −3 ____ 3 ____ −3 ____ 3 ____ −3 ____ −3

4 ____ −3 ____ 3 ____ 3 ____ −3 ____ −3 ____ 3 ____ −3 ____ −3

5 ____ 3 ____ −3 ____ −3 ____ 3 ____ −3 ____ 3 ____ −3 ____ 3

6 ____ −3 ____ 3 ____ 3 ____ −3 ____ 3 ____ −3 ____ 3 ____ 3

7 ____ 3 ____ −3 ____ 3 ____ 3 ____ −3 ____ 3 ____ −3 ____ −3

8 ____ 3 ____ −3 ____ 3 ____ −3 ____ 3 ____ −3 ____ 3 ____ −3

9 ____ −3 ____ −3 ____ 3 ____ −3 ____ 3 ____ −3 ____ −3 ____ −3

10 ____ 3 ____ −3 ____ 3 ____ 3 ____ −3 ____ 3 ____ −3 ____ −3

11 ____ −3 ____ −3 ____ −3 ____ −3 ____ 3 ____ −3 ____ −3 ____ 3

12 ____ −3 ____ 3 ____ −3 ____ −3 ____ 3 ____ −3 ____ 3 ____ 3

A7-2
(Copy 2)

Harmonic interval identification: Major and minor thirds

Shield the answer. Listen to the interval and write 3 or −3 in the blank; then uncover the answer and compare your response. Circle incorrect responses. Goal: No more than twelve errors.

1 ____ 3 ____ −3 ____ 3 ____ −3 ____ −3 ____ 3 ____ −3 ____ 3

2 ____ 3 ____ −3 ____ −3 ____ 3 ____ 3 ____ −3 ____ −3 ____ 3

3 ____ 3 ____ −3 ____ −3 ____ 3 ____ −3 ____ 3 ____ −3 ____ −3

4 ____ −3 ____ 3 ____ 3 ____ −3 ____ −3 ____ 3 ____ −3 ____ −3

5 ____ 3 ____ −3 ____ −3 ____ 3 ____ −3 ____ 3 ____ −3 ____ 3

6 ____ −3 ____ 3 ____ 3 ____ −3 ____ 3 ____ −3 ____ 3 ____ 3

7 ____ 3 ____ −3 ____ 3 ____ 3 ____ −3 ____ 3 ____ −3 ____ −3

8 ____ 3 ____ −3 ____ 3 ____ −3 ____ 3 ____ −3 ____ 3 ____ −3

9 ____ −3 ____ −3 ____ 3 ____ −3 ____ 3 ____ −3 ____ −3 ____ −3

10 ____ 3 ____ −3 ____ 3 ____ 3 ____ −3 ____ 3 ____ −3 ____ −3

11 ____ −3 ____ −3 ____ −3 ____ −3 ____ 3 ____ −3 ____ −3 ____ 3

12 ____ −3 ____ 3 ____ −3 ____ −3 ____ 3 ____ −3 ____ 3 ____ 3

A7-2
(Copy 3)

Harmonic interval identification: Major and minor thirds

Shield the answer. Listen to the interval and write 3 or −3 in the blank; then uncover the answer and compare your response. Circle incorrect responses. Goal: No more than twelve errors.

1 ___ 3 ___ −3 ___ 3 ___ −3 ___ −3 ___ 3 ___ −3 ___ 3
2 ___ 3 ___ −3 ___ −3 ___ 3 ___ 3 ___ −3 ___ −3 ___ 3
3 ___ 3 ___ −3 ___ −3 ___ 3 ___ −3 ___ 3 ___ −3 ___ −3
4 ___ −3 ___ 3 ___ 3 ___ −3 ___ −3 ___ 3 ___ −3 ___ −3
5 ___ 3 ___ −3 ___ −3 ___ 3 ___ −3 ___ 3 ___ −3 ___ 3
6 ___ −3 ___ 3 ___ 3 ___ −3 ___ 3 ___ −3 ___ 3 ___ 3
7 ___ 3 ___ −3 ___ 3 ___ 3 ___ −3 ___ 3 ___ −3 ___ −3
8 ___ 3 ___ −3 ___ 3 ___ −3 ___ 3 ___ −3 ___ 3 ___ −3
9 ___ −3 ___ −3 ___ 3 ___ −3 ___ 3 ___ −3 ___ −3 ___ −3
10 ___ 3 ___ −3 ___ 3 ___ 3 ___ −3 ___ 3 ___ −3 ___ −3
11 ___ −3 ___ −3 ___ −3 ___ −3 ___ 3 ___ −3 ___ −3 ___ 3
12 ___ −3 ___ 3 ___ −3 ___ −3 ___ 3 ___ −3 ___ 3 ___ 3

A7-2
(Copy 4)

Harmonic interval identification: Major and minor thirds

Shield the answer. Listen to the interval and write 3 or −3 in the blank; then uncover the answer and compare your response. Circle incorrect responses. Goal: No more than twelve errors.

1 ___ 3 ___ −3 ___ 3 ___ −3 ___ −3 ___ 3 ___ −3 ___ 3
2 ___ 3 ___ −3 ___ −3 ___ 3 ___ 3 ___ −3 ___ −3 ___ 3
3 ___ 3 ___ −3 ___ −3 ___ 3 ___ −3 ___ 3 ___ −3 ___ −3
4 ___ −3 ___ 3 ___ 3 ___ −3 ___ −3 ___ 3 ___ −3 ___ −3
5 ___ 3 ___ −3 ___ −3 ___ 3 ___ −3 ___ 3 ___ −3 ___ 3
6 ___ −3 ___ 3 ___ 3 ___ −3 ___ 3 ___ −3 ___ 3 ___ 3
7 ___ 3 ___ −3 ___ 3 ___ 3 ___ −3 ___ 3 ___ −3 ___ −3
8 ___ 3 ___ −3 ___ 3 ___ −3 ___ 3 ___ −3 ___ 3 ___ −3
9 ___ −3 ___ −3 ___ 3 ___ −3 ___ 3 ___ −3 ___ −3 ___ −3
10 ___ 3 ___ −3 ___ 3 ___ 3 ___ −3 ___ 3 ___ −3 ___ −3
11 ___ −3 ___ −3 ___ −3 ___ −3 ___ 3 ___ −3 ___ −3 ___ 3
12 ___ −3 ___ 3 ___ −3 ___ −3 ___ 3 ___ −3 ___ 3 ___ 3

A7-2
(Copy 5)

Harmonic interval identification: Major and minor thirds

Shield the answer. Listen to the interval and write 3 or −3 in the blank; then uncover the answer and compare your response. Circle incorrect responses. Goal: No more than twelve errors.

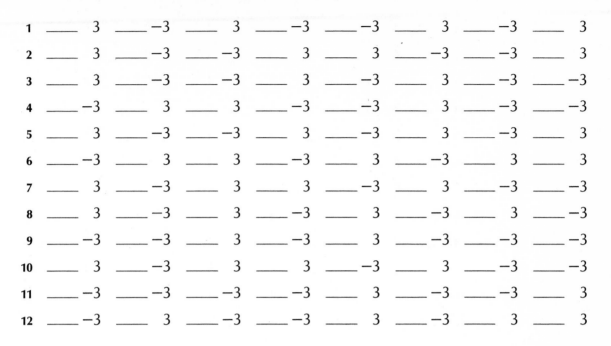

1   ___ 3   ___−3   ___ 3   ___−3   ___−3   ___ 3   ___−3   ___ 3

2   ___ 3   ___−3   ___−3   ___ 3   ___ 3   ___−3   ___−3   ___ 3

3   ___ 3   ___−3   ___−3   ___ 3   ___−3   ___ 3   ___−3   ___−3

4   ___−3   ___ 3   ___ 3   ___−3   ___−3   ___ 3   ___−3   ___−3

5   ___ 3   ___−3   ___−3   ___ 3   ___−3   ___ 3   ___−3   ___ 3

6   ___−3   ___ 3   ___ 3   ___−3   ___ 3   ___−3   ___ 3   ___ 3

7   ___ 3   ___−3   ___ 3   ___ 3   ___−3   ___ 3   ___−3   ___−3

8   ___ 3   ___−3   ___ 3   ___−3   ___ 3   ___−3   ___ 3   ___−3

9   ___−3   ___−3   ___ 3   ___−3   ___ 3   ___−3   ___−3   ___−3

10   ___ 3   ___−3   ___ 3   ___ 3   ___−3   ___ 3   ___−3   ___−3

11   ___−3   ___−3   ___−3   ___−3   ___ 3   ___−3   ___−3   ___ 3

12   ___−3   ___ 3   ___−3   ___−3   ___ 3   ___−3   ___ 3   ___ 3

A7-3
(Copy 1)

Harmonic interval identification: Perfect fourths and fifths

Shield the answer. Listen to the interval and write 4 or 5 in the blank; then uncover the answer and compare your response. Circle incorrect responses. Goal: No more than twelve errors.

1 ___ 5 ___ 4 ___ 5 ___ 4 ___ 4 ___ 5 ___ 4 ___ 5

2 ___ 4 ___ 5 ___ 4 ___ 5 ___ 4 ___ 5 ___ 4 ___ 5

3 ___ 5 ___ 4 ___ 5 ___ 4 ___ 5 ___ 4 ___ 5 ___ 4

4 ___ 5 ___ 4 ___ 5 ___ 5 ___ 4 ___ 5 ___ 4 ___ 5

5 ___ 5 ___ 5 ___ 4 ___ 4 ___ 4 ___ 4 ___ 5 ___ 5

6 ___ 4 ___ 5 ___ 5 ___ 4 ___ 5 ___ 4 ___ 5 ___ 4

7 ___ 5 ___ 5 ___ 4 ___ 5 ___ 5 ___ 5 ___ 4 ___ 4

8 ___ 5 ___ 4 ___ 5 ___ 5 ___ 4 ___ 4 ___ 5 ___ 5

9 ___ 4 ___ 4 ___ 5 ___ 4 ___ 5 ___ 4 ___ 4 ___ 4

10 ___ 5 ___ 4 ___ 4 ___ 5 ___ 5 ___ 4 ___ 4 ___ 5

11 ___ 5 ___ 5 ___ 4 ___ 4 ___ 5 ___ 4 ___ 5 ___ 4

12 ___ 4 ___ 5 ___ 4 ___ 5 ___ 4 ___ 5 ___ 5 ___ 4

A7-3
(Copy 2)

Harmonic interval identification: Perfect fourths and fifths

Shield the answer. Listen to the interval and write 4 or 5 in the blank; then uncover the answer and compare your response. Circle incorrect responses. Goal: No more than twelve errors.

1 ___ 5 ___ 4 ___ 5 ___ 4 ___ 4 ___ 5 ___ 4 ___ 5

2 ___ 4 ___ 5 ___ 4 ___ 5 ___ 4 ___ 5 ___ 4 ___ 5

3 ___ 5 ___ 4 ___ 5 ___ 4 ___ 5 ___ 4 ___ 5 ___ 4

4 ___ 5 ___ 4 ___ 5 ___ 5 ___ 4 ___ 5 ___ 4 ___ 5

5 ___ 5 ___ 5 ___ 4 ___ 4 ___ 4 ___ 4 ___ 5 ___ 5

6 ___ 4 ___ 5 ___ 5 ___ 4 ___ 5 ___ 4 ___ 5 ___ 4

7 ___ 5 ___ 5 ___ 4 ___ 5 ___ 5 ___ 5 ___ 4 ___ 4

8 ___ 5 ___ 4 ___ 5 ___ 5 ___ 4 ___ 4 ___ 5 ___ 5

9 ___ 4 ___ 4 ___ 5 ___ 4 ___ 5 ___ 4 ___ 4 ___ 4

10 ___ 5 ___ 4 ___ 4 ___ 5 ___ 5 ___ 4 ___ 4 ___ 5

11 ___ 5 ___ 5 ___ 4 ___ 4 ___ 5 ___ 4 ___ 5 ___ 4

12 ___ 4 ___ 5 ___ 4 ___ 5 ___ 4 ___ 5 ___ 5 ___ 4

A7-3
(Copy 3)

Harmonic interval identification: Perfect fourths and fifths

Shield the answer. Listen to the interval and write 4 or 5 in the blank; then uncover the answer and compare your response. Circle incorrect responses. Goal: No more than twelve errors.

1 ___ 5 ___ 4 ___ 5 ___ 4 ___ 4 ___ 5 ___ 4 ___ 5

2 ___ 4 ___ 5 ___ 4 ___ 5 ___ 4 ___ 5 ___ 4 ___ 5

3 ___ 5 ___ 4 ___ 5 ___ 4 ___ 5 ___ 4 ___ 5 ___ 4

4 ___ 5 ___ 4 ___ 5 ___ 5 ___ 4 ___ 5 ___ 4 ___ 5

5 ___ 5 ___ 5 ___ 4 ___ 4 ___ 4 ___ 4 ___ 5 ___ 5

6 ___ 4 ___ 5 ___ 5 ___ 4 ___ 5 ___ 4 ___ 5 ___ 4

7 ___ 5 ___ 5 ___ 4 ___ 5 ___ 5 ___ 5 ___ 4 ___ 4

8 ___ 5 ___ 4 ___ 5 ___ 5 ___ 4 ___ 4 ___ 5 ___ 5

9 ___ 4 ___ 4 ___ 5 ___ 4 ___ 5 ___ 4 ___ 4 ___ 4

10 ___ 5 ___ 4 ___ 4 ___ 5 ___ 5 ___ 4 ___ 4 ___ 5

11 ___ 5 ___ 5 ___ 4 ___ 4 ___ 5 ___ 4 ___ 5 ___ 4

12 ___ 4 ___ 5 ___ 4 ___ 5 ___ 4 ___ 5 ___ 5 ___ 4

A7-3
(Copy 4)

Harmonic interval identification: Perfect fourths and fifths

Shield the answer. Listen to the interval and write 4 or 5 in the blank; then uncover the answer and compare your response. Circle incorrect responses. Goal: No more than twelve errors.

1 ___ 5 ___ 4 ___ 5 ___ 4 ___ 4 ___ 5 ___ 4 ___ 5

2 ___ 4 ___ 5 ___ 4 ___ 5 ___ 4 ___ 5 ___ 4 ___ 5

3 ___ 5 ___ 4 ___ 5 ___ 4 ___ 5 ___ 4 ___ 5 ___ 4

4 ___ 5 ___ 4 ___ 5 ___ 5 ___ 4 ___ 5 ___ 4 ___ 5

5 ___ 5 ___ 5 ___ 4 ___ 4 ___ 4 ___ 4 ___ 5 ___ 5

6 ___ 4 ___ 5 ___ 5 ___ 4 ___ 5 ___ 4 ___ 5 ___ 4

7 ___ 5 ___ 5 ___ 4 ___ 5 ___ 5 ___ 5 ___ 4 ___ 4

8 ___ 5 ___ 4 ___ 5 ___ 5 ___ 4 ___ 4 ___ 5 ___ 5

9 ___ 4 ___ 4 ___ 5 ___ 4 ___ 5 ___ 4 ___ 4 ___ 4

10 ___ 5 ___ 4 ___ 4 ___ 5 ___ 5 ___ 4 ___ 4 ___ 5

11 ___ 5 ___ 5 ___ 4 ___ 4 ___ 5 ___ 4 ___ 5 ___ 4

12 ___ 4 ___ 5 ___ 4 ___ 5 ___ 4 ___ 5 ___ 5 ___ 4

Harmonic interval identification: Perfect fourths and fifths

Shield the answer. Listen to the interval and write 4 or 5 in the blank; then uncover the answer and compare your response. Circle incorrect responses. Goal: No more than twelve errors.

1 ___ 5 ___ 4 ___ 5 ___ 4 ___ 4 ___ 5 ___ 4 ___ 5

2 ___ 4 ___ 5 ___ 4 ___ 5 ___ 4 ___ 5 ___ 4 ___ 5

3 ___ 5 ___ 4 ___ 5 ___ 4 ___ 5 ___ 4 ___ 5 ___ 4

4 ___ 5 ___ 4 ___ 5 ___ 5 ___ 4 ___ 5 ___ 4 ___ 5

5 ___ 5 ___ 5 ___ 4 ___ 4 ___ 4 ___ 4 ___ 5 ___ 5

6 ___ 4 ___ 5 ___ 5 ___ 4 ___ 5 ___ 4 ___ 5 ___ 4

7 ___ 5 ___ 5 ___ 4 ___ 5 ___ 5 ___ 5 ___ 4 ___ 4

8 ___ 5 ___ 4 ___ 5 ___ 5 ___ 4 ___ 4 ___ 5 ___ 5

9 ___ 4 ___ 4 ___ 5 ___ 4 ___ 5 ___ 4 ___ 4 ___ 4

10 ___ 5 ___ 4 ___ 4 ___ 5 ___ 5 ___ 4 ___ 4 ___ 5

11 ___ 5 ___ 5 ___ 4 ___ 4 ___ 5 ___ 4 ___ 5 ___ 4

12 ___ 4 ___ 5 ___ 4 ___ 5 ___ 4 ___ 5 ___ 5 ___ 4

A7-4
(Copy 1)

Harmonic interval identification: Major and minor sixths

Shield the answer. Listen to the interval and write 6 or −6 in the blank; then uncover the answer and compare your response. Circle incorrect responses. Goal: No more than twelve errors.

1 ___ 6 ___ −6 ___ −6 ___ 6 ___ 6 ___ −6 ___ −6 ___ 6
2 ___ 6 ___ −6 ___ 6 ___ −6 ___ −6 ___ 6 ___ −6 ___ 6
3 ___ −6 ___ 6 ___ 6 ___ −6 ___ 6 ___ −6 ___ −6 ___ 6
4 ___ −6 ___ 6 ___ 6 ___ −6 ___ 6 ___ −6 ___ −6 ___ 6
5 ___ −6 ___ 6 ___ 6 ___ −6 ___ −6 ___ −6 ___ 6 ___ 6
6 ___ 6 ___ −6 ___ −6 ___ 6 ___ 6 ___ −6 ___ −6 ___ 6
7 ___ −6 ___ −6 ___ 6 ___ 6 ___ 6 ___ 6 ___ −6 ___ −6
8 ___ 6 ___ −6 ___ 6 ___ 6 ___ −6 ___ −6 ___ −6 ___ 6
9 ___ −6 ___ 6 ___ −6 ___ 6 ___ −6 ___ 6 ___ 6 ___ 6
10 ___ 6 ___ −6 ___ 6 ___ 6 ___ −6 ___ 6 ___ 6 ___ −6
11 ___ 6 ___ 6 ___ −6 ___ −6 ___ 6 ___ −6 ___ 6 ___ −6
12 ___ 6 ___ 6 ___ −6 ___ −6 ___ −6 ___ 6 ___ 6 ___ −6

A7-4
(Copy 2)

Harmonic interval identification: Major and minor sixths

Shield the answer. Listen to the interval and write 6 or −6 in the blank; then uncover the answer and compare your response. Circle incorrect responses. Goal: No more than twelve errors.

1 ___ 6 ___ −6 ___ −6 ___ 6 ___ 6 ___ −6 ___ −6 ___ 6
2 ___ 6 ___ −6 ___ 6 ___ −6 ___ −6 ___ 6 ___ −6 ___ 6
3 ___ −6 ___ 6 ___ 6 ___ −6 ___ 6 ___ −6 ___ −6 ___ 6
4 ___ −6 ___ 6 ___ 6 ___ −6 ___ 6 ___ −6 ___ −6 ___ 6
5 ___ −6 ___ 6 ___ 6 ___ −6 ___ −6 ___ −6 ___ 6 ___ 6
6 ___ 6 ___ −6 ___ −6 ___ 6 ___ 6 ___ −6 ___ −6 ___ 6
7 ___ −6 ___ −6 ___ 6 ___ 6 ___ 6 ___ 6 ___ −6 ___ −6
8 ___ 6 ___ −6 ___ 6 ___ 6 ___ −6 ___ −6 ___ −6 ___ 6
9 ___ −6 ___ 6 ___ −6 ___ 6 ___ −6 ___ 6 ___ 6 ___ 6
10 ___ 6 ___ −6 ___ 6 ___ 6 ___ −6 ___ 6 ___ 6 ___ −6
11 ___ 6 ___ 6 ___ −6 ___ −6 ___ 6 ___ −6 ___ 6 ___ −6
12 ___ 6 ___ 6 ___ −6 ___ −6 ___ −6 ___ 6 ___ 6 ___ −6

A7-4
(Copy 3)

Harmonic interval identification: Major and minor sixths

Shield the answer. Listen to the interval and write 6 or −6 in the blank; then uncover the answer and compare your response. Circle incorrect responses. Goal: No more than twelve errors.

1. ___ 6   ___ −6   ___ −6   ___ 6   ___ 6   ___ −6   ___ −6   ___ 6
2. ___ 6   ___ −6   ___ 6   ___ −6   ___ −6   ___ 6   ___ −6   ___ 6
3. ___ −6   ___ 6   ___ 6   ___ −6   ___ 6   ___ −6   ___ −6   ___ 6
4. ___ −6   ___ 6   ___ 6   ___ −6   ___ 6   ___ −6   ___ −6   ___ 6
5. ___ −6   ___ 6   ___ 6   ___ −6   ___ −6   ___ −6   ___ 6   ___ 6
6. ___ 6   ___ −6   ___ −6   ___ 6   ___ 6   ___ −6   ___ −6   ___ 6
7. ___ −6   ___ −6   ___ 6   ___ 6   ___ 6   ___ 6   ___ −6   ___ −6
8. ___ 6   ___ −6   ___ 6   ___ 6   ___ −6   ___ −6   ___ −6   ___ 6
9. ___ −6   ___ 6   ___ −6   ___ 6   ___ −6   ___ 6   ___ 6   ___ 6
10. ___ 6   ___ −6   ___ 6   ___ 6   ___ −6   ___ 6   ___ 6   ___ −6
11. ___ 6   ___ 6   ___ −6   ___ −6   ___ 6   ___ −6   ___ 6   ___ −6
12. ___ 6   ___ 6   ___ −6   ___ −6   ___ −6   ___ 6   ___ 6   ___ −6

A7-4
(Copy 4)

Harmonic interval identification: Major and minor sixths

Shield the answer. Listen to the interval and write 6 or −6 in the blank; then uncover the answer and compare your response. Circle incorrect responses. Goal: No more than twelve errors.

1. ___ 6   ___ −6   ___ −6   ___ 6   ___ 6   ___ −6   ___ −6   ___ 6
2. ___ 6   ___ −6   ___ 6   ___ −6   ___ −6   ___ 6   ___ −6   ___ 6
3. ___ −6   ___ 6   ___ 6   ___ −6   ___ 6   ___ −6   ___ −6   ___ 6
4. ___ −6   ___ 6   ___ 6   ___ −6   ___ 6   ___ −6   ___ −6   ___ 6
5. ___ −6   ___ 6   ___ 6   ___ −6   ___ −6   ___ −6   ___ 6   ___ 6
6. ___ 6   ___ −6   ___ −6   ___ 6   ___ 6   ___ −6   ___ −6   ___ 6
7. ___ −6   ___ −6   ___ 6   ___ 6   ___ 6   ___ 6   ___ −6   ___ −6
8. ___ 6   ___ −6   ___ 6   ___ 6   ___ −6   ___ −6   ___ −6   ___ 6
9. ___ −6   ___ 6   ___ −6   ___ 6   ___ −6   ___ 6   ___ 6   ___ 6
10. ___ 6   ___ −6   ___ 6   ___ 6   ___ −6   ___ 6   ___ 6   ___ −6
11. ___ 6   ___ 6   ___ −6   ___ −6   ___ 6   ___ −6   ___ 6   ___ −6
12. ___ 6   ___ 6   ___ −6   ___ −6   ___ −6   ___ 6   ___ 6   ___ −6

Harmonic interval identification: Major and minor sixths

Shield the answer. Listen to the interval and write 6 or −6 in the blank; then uncover the answer and compare your response. Circle incorrect responses. Goal: No more than twelve errors.

1 ___ 6 ___ −6 ___ −6 ___ 6 ___ 6 ___ −6 ___ −6 ___ 6

2 ___ 6 ___ −6 ___ 6 ___ −6 ___ −6 ___ 6 ___ −6 ___ 6

3 ___ −6 ___ 6 ___ 6 ___ −6 ___ 6 ___ −6 ___ −6 ___ 6

4 ___ −6 ___ 6 ___ 6 ___ −6 ___ 6 ___ −6 ___ −6 ___ 6

5 ___ −6 ___ 6 ___ 6 ___ −6 ___ −6 ___ −6 ___ 6 ___ 6

6 ___ 6 ___ −6 ___ −6 ___ 6 ___ 6 ___ −6 ___ −6 ___ 6

7 ___ −6 ___ −6 ___ 6 ___ 6 ___ 6 ___ 6 ___ −6 ___ −6

8 ___ 6 ___ −6 ___ 6 ___ 6 ___ −6 ___ −6 ___ −6 ___ 6

9 ___ −6 ___ 6 ___ −6 ___ 6 ___ −6 ___ 6 ___ 6 ___ 6

10 ___ 6 ___ −6 ___ 6 ___ 6 ___ −6 ___ 6 ___ 6 ___ −6

11 ___ 6 ___ 6 ___ −6 ___ −6 ___ 6 ___ −6 ___ 6 ___ −6

12 ___ 6 ___ 6 ___ −6 ___ −6 ___ −6 ___ 6 ___ 6 ___ −6

A7-5
(Copy 1)

Harmonic interval identification: Tritones, major and minor sevenths, perfect octaves

Shield the answer. Listen to the interval and write T, 7, −7, or 8 in the blank; then uncover the answer and compare your response. Circle incorrect responses. Goal: No more than twelve errors.

1 ___ 8 ___ 7 ___ −7 ___ 8 ___ −7 ___ 7 ___ T ___ −7
2 ___ −7 ___ 7 ___ 7 ___ −7 ___ −7 ___ 7 ___ T ___ T
3 ___ T ___ 7 ___ −7 ___ 8 ___ T ___ 7 ___ 8 ___ −7
4 ___ 8 ___ 7 ___ T ___ −7 ___ −7 ___ 7 ___ T ___ −7
5 ___ 7 ___ −7 ___ T ___ 7 ___ −7 ___ 7 ___ 8 ___ T
6 ___ 8 ___ 7 ___ −7 ___ T ___ −7 ___ 7 ___ 7 ___ T
7 ___ 7 ___ T ___ −7 ___ −7 ___ T ___ 7 ___ 7 ___ −7
8 ___ 7 ___ −7 ___ T ___ −7 ___ T ___ 7 ___ T ___ 7
9 ___ −7 ___ 7 ___ T ___ −7 ___ T ___ 7 ___ −7 ___ −7
10 ___ 7 ___ −7 ___ 7 ___ 7 ___ −7 ___ −7 ___ −7 ___ 7
11 ___ −7 ___ 7 ___ −7 ___ −7 ___ −7 ___ 7 ___ −7 ___ −7
12 ___ 7 ___ −7 ___ −7 ___ 7 ___ 7 ___ −7 ___ 7 ___ 7

A7-5
(Copy 2)

Harmonic interval identification: Tritones, major and minor sevenths, perfect octaves

Shield the answer. Listen to the interval and write T, 7, −7, or 8 in the blank; then uncover the answer and compare your response. Circle incorrect responses. Goal: No more than twelve errors.

1 ___ 8 ___ 7 ___ −7 ___ 8 ___ −7 ___ 7 ___ T ___ −7
2 ___ −7 ___ 7 ___ 7 ___ −7 ___ −7 ___ 7 ___ T ___ T
3 ___ T ___ 7 ___ −7 ___ 8 ___ T ___ 7 ___ 8 ___ −7
4 ___ 8 ___ 7 ___ T ___ −7 ___ −7 ___ 7 ___ T ___ −7
5 ___ 7 ___ −7 ___ T ___ 7 ___ −7 ___ 7 ___ 8 ___ T
6 ___ 8 ___ 7 ___ −7 ___ T ___ −7 ___ 7 ___ 7 ___ T
7 ___ 7 ___ T ___ −7 ___ −7 ___ T ___ 7 ___ 7 ___ −7
8 ___ 7 ___ −7 ___ T ___ −7 ___ T ___ 7 ___ T ___ 7
9 ___ −7 ___ 7 ___ T ___ −7 ___ T ___ 7 ___ −7 ___ −7
10 ___ 7 ___ −7 ___ 7 ___ 7 ___ −7 ___ −7 ___ −7 ___ 7
11 ___ −7 ___ 7 ___ −7 ___ −7 ___ −7 ___ 7 ___ −7 ___ −7
12 ___ 7 ___ −7 ___ −7 ___ 7 ___ 7 ___ −7 ___ 7 ___ 7

A7–5
(Copy 3)

Harmonic interval identification: Tritones, major and minor sevenths, perfect octaves

Shield the answer. Listen to the interval and write T, 7, −7, or 8 in the blank; then uncover the answer and compare your response. Circle incorrect responses. Goal: No more than twelve errors.

1. ___ 8 ___ 7 ___ −7 ___ 8 ___ −7 ___ 7 ___ T ___ −7
2. ___ −7 ___ 7 ___ 7 ___ −7 ___ −7 ___ 7 ___ T ___ T
3. ___ T ___ 7 ___ −7 ___ 8 ___ T ___ 7 ___ 8 ___ −7
4. ___ 8 ___ 7 ___ T ___ −7 ___ −7 ___ 7 ___ T ___ −7
5. ___ 7 ___ −7 ___ T ___ 7 ___ −7 ___ 7 ___ 8 ___ T
6. ___ 8 ___ 7 ___ −7 ___ T ___ −7 ___ 7 ___ 7 ___ T
7. ___ 7 ___ T ___ −7 ___ −7 ___ T ___ 7 ___ 7 ___ −7
8. ___ 7 ___ −7 ___ T ___ −7 ___ T ___ 7 ___ T ___ 7
9. ___ −7 ___ 7 ___ T ___ −7 ___ T ___ 7 ___ −7 ___ −7
10. ___ 7 ___ −7 ___ 7 ___ 7 ___ −7 ___ −7 ___ −7 ___ 7
11. ___ −7 ___ 7 ___ −7 ___ −7 ___ −7 ___ 7 ___ −7 ___ −7
12. ___ 7 ___ −7 ___ −7 ___ 7 ___ 7 ___ −7 ___ 7 ___ 7

A7–5
(Copy 4)

Harmonic interval identification: Tritones, major and minor sevenths, perfect octaves

Shield the answer. Listen to the interval and write T, 7, −7, or 8 in the blank; then uncover the answer and compare your response. Circle incorrect responses. Goal: No more than twelve errors.

1. ___ 8 ___ 7 ___ −7 ___ 8 ___ −7 ___ 7 ___ T ___ −7
2. ___ −7 ___ 7 ___ 7 ___ −7 ___ −7 ___ 7 ___ T ___ T
3. ___ T ___ 7 ___ −7 ___ 8 ___ T ___ 7 ___ 8 ___ −7
4. ___ 8 ___ 7 ___ T ___ −7 ___ −7 ___ 7 ___ T ___ −7
5. ___ 7 ___ −7 ___ T ___ 7 ___ −7 ___ 7 ___ 8 ___ T
6. ___ 8 ___ 7 ___ −7 ___ T ___ −7 ___ 7 ___ 7 ___ T
7. ___ 7 ___ T ___ −7 ___ −7 ___ T ___ 7 ___ 7 ___ −7
8. ___ 7 ___ −7 ___ T ___ −7 ___ T ___ 7 ___ T ___ 7
9. ___ −7 ___ 7 ___ T ___ −7 ___ T ___ 7 ___ −7 ___ −7
10. ___ 7 ___ −7 ___ 7 ___ 7 ___ −7 ___ −7 ___ −7 ___ 7
11. ___ −7 ___ 7 ___ −7 ___ −7 ___ −7 ___ 7 ___ −7 ___ −7
12. ___ 7 ___ −7 ___ −7 ___ 7 ___ 7 ___ −7 ___ 7 ___ 7

Harmonic interval identification: Tritones, major and minor sevenths, perfect octaves

Shield the answer. Listen to the interval and write T, 7, −7, or 8 in the blank; then uncover the answer and compare your response. Circle incorrect responses. Goal: No more than twelve errors.

1	___ 8	___ 7	___ −7	___ 8	___ −7	___ 7	___ T	___ −7
2	___ −7	___ 7	___ 7	___ −7	___ −7	___ 7	___ T	___ T
3	___ T	___ 7	___ −7	___ 8	___ T	___ 7	___ 8	___ −7
4	___ 8	___ 7	___ T	___ −7	___ −7	___ 7	___ T	___ −7
5	___ 7	___ −7	___ T	___ 7	___ −7	___ 7	___ 8	___ T
6	___ 8	___ 7	___ −7	___ T	___ −7	___ 7	___ 7	___ T
7	___ 7	___ T	___ −7	___ −7	___ T	___ 7	___ 7	___ −7
8	___ 7	___ −7	___ T	___ −7	___ T	___ 7	___ T	___ 7
9	___ −7	___ 7	___ T	___ −7	___ T	___ 7	___ −7	___ −7
10	___ 7	___ −7	___ 7	___ 7	___ −7	___ −7	___ −7	___ 7
11	___ −7	___ 7	___ −7	___ −7	___ −7	___ 7	___ −7	___ −7
12	___ 7	___ −7	___ −7	___ 7	___ 7	___ −7	___ 7	___ 7

A7-6
(Copy 1)

Harmonic interval identification: Major and minor thirds, major and minor sixths

Shield the answer. Listen to the interval and write 3, −3, 6, or −6 in the blank; then uncover the answer and compare your response. Circle incorrect responses. Goal: No more than twelve errors.

1 ____ 3 ____ −3 ____ 6 ____ −6 ____ −6 ____ 6 ____ 3 ____ −3

2 ____ −3 ____ 3 ____ 6 ____ −6 ____ −6 ____ −3 ____ 3 ____ 6

3 ____ −3 ____ 6 ____ −6 ____ 3 ____ 3 ____ −6 ____ −3 ____ 6

4 ____ 6 ____ 3 ____ −6 ____ −3 ____ −6 ____ −3 ____ 3 ____ 6

5 ____ −3 ____ 6 ____ 3 ____ −6 ____ 3 ____ −6 ____ −3 ____ 6

6 ____ 6 ____ 3 ____ −6 ____ −3 ____ 3 ____ −6 ____ −3 ____ 6

7 ____ 6 ____ −3 ____ −6 ____ 3 ____ −6 ____ 3 ____ −3 ____ 6

8 ____ −3 ____ 6 ____ 3 ____ 3 ____ 6 ____ −6 ____ −3 ____ 6

9 ____ −6 ____ 3 ____ 6 ____ 3 ____ −6 ____ −3 ____ 6 ____ 6

10 ____ 3 ____ −6 ____ −6 ____ 3 ____ −3 ____ 6 ____ 6 ____ 3

11 ____ 6 ____ 3 ____ −6 ____ −3 ____ 6 ____ −6 ____ −3 ____ 3

12 ____ 6 ____ −3 ____ 6 ____ −3 ____ 3 ____ 3 ____ 6 ____ −6

A7-6
(Copy 2)

Harmonic interval identification: Major and minor thirds, major and minor sixths

Shield the answer. Listen to the interval and write 3, −3, 6, or −6 in the blank; then uncover the answer and compare your response. Circle incorrect responses. Goal: No more than twelve errors.

1 ____ 3 ____ −3 ____ 6 ____ −6 ____ −6 ____ 6 ____ 3 ____ −3

2 ____ −3 ____ 3 ____ 6 ____ −6 ____ −6 ____ −3 ____ 3 ____ 6

3 ____ −3 ____ 6 ____ −6 ____ 3 ____ 3 ____ −6 ____ −3 ____ 6

4 ____ 6 ____ 3 ____ −6 ____ −3 ____ −6 ____ −3 ____ 3 ____ 6

5 ____ −3 ____ 6 ____ 3 ____ −6 ____ 3 ____ −6 ____ −3 ____ 6

6 ____ 6 ____ 3 ____ −6 ____ −3 ____ 3 ____ −6 ____ −3 ____ 6

7 ____ 6 ____ −3 ____ −6 ____ 3 ____ −6 ____ 3 ____ −3 ____ 6

8 ____ −3 ____ 6 ____ 3 ____ 3 ____ 6 ____ −6 ____ −3 ____ 6

9 ____ −6 ____ 3 ____ 6 ____ 3 ____ −6 ____ −3 ____ 6 ____ 6

10 ____ 3 ____ −6 ____ −6 ____ 3 ____ −3 ____ 6 ____ 6 ____ 3

11 ____ 6 ____ 3 ____ −6 ____ −3 ____ 6 ____ −6 ____ −3 ____ 3

12 ____ 6 ____ −3 ____ 6 ____ −3 ____ 3 ____ 3 ____ 6 ____ −6

A7-6
(Copy 3)

Harmonic interval identification: Major and minor thirds, major and minor sixths

Shield the answer. Listen to the interval and write 3, −3, 6, or −6 in the blank; then uncover the answer and compare your response. Circle incorrect responses. Goal: No more than twelve errors.

1 ___ 3 ___ −3 ___ 6 ___ −6 ___ −6 ___ 6 ___ 3 ___ −3
2 ___ −3 ___ 3 ___ 6 ___ −6 ___ −6 ___ −3 ___ 3 ___ 6
3 ___ −3 ___ 6 ___ −6 ___ 3 ___ 3 ___ −6 ___ −3 ___ 6
4 ___ 6 ___ 3 ___ −6 ___ −3 ___ −6 ___ −3 ___ 3 ___ 6
5 ___ −3 ___ 6 ___ 3 ___ −6 ___ 3 ___ −6 ___ −3 ___ 6
6 ___ 6 ___ 3 ___ −6 ___ −3 ___ 3 ___ −6 ___ −3 ___ 6
7 ___ 6 ___ −3 ___ −6 ___ 3 ___ −6 ___ 3 ___ −3 ___ 6
8 ___ −3 ___ 6 ___ 3 ___ 3 ___ 6 ___ −6 ___ −3 ___ 6
9 ___ −6 ___ 3 ___ 6 ___ 3 ___ −6 ___ −3 ___ 6 ___ 6
10 ___ 3 ___ −6 ___ −6 ___ 3 ___ −3 ___ 6 ___ 6 ___ 3
11 ___ 6 ___ 3 ___ −6 ___ −3 ___ 6 ___ −6 ___ −3 ___ 3
12 ___ 6 ___ −3 ___ 6 ___ −3 ___ 3 ___ 3 ___ 6 ___ −6

A7-6
(Copy 4)

Harmonic interval identification: Major and minor thirds, major and minor sixths

Shield the answer. Listen to the interval and write 3, −3, 6, or −6 in the blank; then uncover the answer and compare your response. Circle incorrect responses. Goal: No more than twelve errors.

1 ___ 3 ___ −3 ___ 6 ___ −6 ___ −6 ___ 6 ___ 3 ___ −3
2 ___ −3 ___ 3 ___ 6 ___ −6 ___ −6 ___ −3 ___ 3 ___ 6
3 ___ −3 ___ 6 ___ −6 ___ 3 ___ 3 ___ −6 ___ −3 ___ 6
4 ___ 6 ___ 3 ___ −6 ___ −3 ___ −6 ___ −3 ___ 3 ___ 6
5 ___ −3 ___ 6 ___ 3 ___ −6 ___ 3 ___ −6 ___ −3 ___ 6
6 ___ 6 ___ 3 ___ −6 ___ −3 ___ 3 ___ −6 ___ −3 ___ 6
7 ___ 6 ___ −3 ___ −6 ___ 3 ___ −6 ___ 3 ___ −3 ___ 6
8 ___ −3 ___ 6 ___ 3 ___ 3 ___ 6 ___ −6 ___ −3 ___ 6
9 ___ −6 ___ 3 ___ 6 ___ 3 ___ −6 ___ −3 ___ 6 ___ 6
10 ___ 3 ___ −6 ___ −6 ___ 3 ___ −3 ___ 6 ___ 6 ___ 3
11 ___ 6 ___ 3 ___ −6 ___ −3 ___ 6 ___ −6 ___ −3 ___ 3
12 ___ 6 ___ −3 ___ 6 ___ −3 ___ 3 ___ 3 ___ 6 ___ −6

Harmonic interval identification: Major and minor thirds, major and minor sixths

Shield the answer. Listen to the interval and write 3, −3, 6, or −6 in the blank; then uncover the answer and compare your response. Circle incorrect responses. Goal: No more than twelve errors.

1   ___ 3   ___ −3   ___ 6   ___ −6   ___ −6   ___ 6   ___ 3   ___ −3

2   ___ −3   ___ 3   ___ 6   ___ −6   ___ −6   ___ −3   ___ 3   ___ 6

3   ___ −3   ___ 6   ___ −6   ___ 3   ___ 3   ___ −6   ___ −3   ___ 6

4   ___ 6   ___ 3   ___ −6   ___ −3   ___ −6   ___ −3   ___ 3   ___ 6

5   ___ −3   ___ 6   ___ 3   ___ −6   ___ 3   ___ −6   ___ −3   ___ 6

6   ___ 6   ___ 3   ___ −6   ___ −3   ___ 3   ___ −6   ___ −3   ___ 6

7   ___ 6   ___ −3   ___ −6   ___ 3   ___ −6   ___ 3   ___ −3   ___ 6

8   ___ −3   ___ 6   ___ 3   ___ 3   ___ 6   ___ −6   ___ −3   ___ 6

9   ___ −6   ___ 3   ___ 6   ___ 3   ___ −6   ___ −3   ___ 6   ___ 6

10 ___ 3   ___ −6   ___ −6   ___ 3   ___ −3   ___ 6   ___ 6   ___ 3

11 ___ 6   ___ 3   ___ −6   ___ −3   ___ 6   ___ −6   ___ −3   ___ 3

12 ___ 6   ___ −3   ___ 6   ___ −3   ___ 3   ___ 3   ___ 6   ___ −6

A7-7
(Copy 1)

Harmonic interval identification: Major and minor seconds, tritones, major and minor sevenths

Shield the answer. Listen to the interval and write 2, −2, T, 7, or −7 in the blank; then uncover the answer and compare your response. Circle incorrect responses. Goal: No more than twelve errors.

1   ___ −2   ___ 2   ___ −7   ___ 7   ___ T   ___ −2   ___ −7   ___ T

2   ___ 7   ___ −7   ___ 2   ___ −2   ___ 7   ___ −7   ___ T   ___ 2

3   ___ 2   ___ −2   ___ −2   ___ 2   ___ 7   ___ −7   ___ T   ___ 7

4   ___ −7   ___ 2   ___ 7   ___ −2   ___ −2   ___ 7   ___ 2   ___ −7

5   ___ −7   ___ 2   ___ 7   ___ −2   ___ 7   ___ −2   ___ 2   ___ −7

6   ___ T   ___ −7   ___ −7   ___ 2   ___ 2   ___ −7   ___ 7   ___ −2

7   ___ 7   ___ −2   ___ −2   ___ 7   ___ T   ___ −7   ___ T   ___ 7

8   ___ −7   ___ 2   ___ 7   ___ −2   ___ 7   ___ −2   ___ −7   ___ 2

9   ___ T   ___ −7   ___ T   ___ −7   ___ 7   ___ −2   ___ 2   ___ −7

10   ___ T   ___ −7   ___ 7   ___ −2   ___ 2   ___ 7   ___ 7   ___ −7

11   ___ T   ___ 7   ___ −7   ___ 7   ___ −2   ___ T   ___ −7   ___ 7

12   ___ −2   ___ −7   ___ T   ___ −7   ___ −7   ___ 7   ___ −2   ___ 7

A7-7
(Copy 2)

Harmonic interval identification: Major and minor seconds, tritones, major and minor sevenths

Shield the answer. Listen to the interval and write 2, −2, T, 7, or −7 in the blank; then uncover the answer and compare your response. Circle incorrect responses. Goal: No more than twelve errors.

1   ___ −2   ___ 2   ___ −7   ___ 7   ___ T   ___ −2   ___ −7   ___ T

2   ___ 7   ___ −7   ___ 2   ___ −2   ___ 7   ___ −7   ___ T   ___ 2

3   ___ 2   ___ −2   ___ −2   ___ 2   ___ 7   ___ −7   ___ T   ___ 7

4   ___ −7   ___ 2   ___ 7   ___ −2   ___ −2   ___ 7   ___ 2   ___ −7

5   ___ −7   ___ 2   ___ 7   ___ −2   ___ 7   ___ −2   ___ 2   ___ −7

6   ___ T   ___ −7   ___ −7   ___ 2   ___ 2   ___ −7   ___ 7   ___ −2

7   ___ 7   ___ −2   ___ −2   ___ 7   ___ T   ___ −7   ___ T   ___ 7

8   ___ −7   ___ 2   ___ 7   ___ −2   ___ 7   ___ −2   ___ −7   ___ 2

9   ___ T   ___ −7   ___ T   ___ −7   ___ 7   ___ −2   ___ 2   ___ −7

10   ___ T   ___ −7   ___ 7   ___ −2   ___ 2   ___ 7   ___ 7   ___ −7

11   ___ T   ___ 7   ___ −7   ___ 7   ___ −2   ___ T   ___ −7   ___ 7

12   ___ −2   ___ −7   ___ T   ___ −7   ___ −7   ___ 7   ___ −2   ___ 7

A7-7
(Copy 3)

Harmonic interval identification: Major and minor seconds, tritones, major and minor sevenths

Shield the answer. Listen to the interval and write 2, −2, T, 7, or −7 in the blank; then uncover the answer and compare your response. Circle incorrect responses. Goal: No more than twelve errors.

1 ___ −2 ___ 2 ___ −7 ___ 7 ___ T ___ −2 ___ −7 ___ T
2 ___ 7 ___ −7 ___ 2 ___ −2 ___ 7 ___ −7 ___ T ___ 2
3 ___ 2 ___ −2 ___ −2 ___ 2 ___ 7 ___ −7 ___ T ___ 7
4 ___ −7 ___ 2 ___ 7 ___ −2 ___ −2 ___ 7 ___ 2 ___ −7
5 ___ −7 ___ 2 ___ 7 ___ −2 ___ 7 ___ −2 ___ 2 ___ −7
6 ___ T ___ −7 ___ −7 ___ 2 ___ 2 ___ −7 ___ 7 ___ −2
7 ___ 7 ___ −2 ___ −2 ___ 7 ___ T ___ −7 ___ T ___ 7
8 ___ −7 ___ 2 ___ 7 ___ −2 ___ 7 ___ −2 ___ −7 ___ 2
9 ___ T ___ −7 ___ T ___ −7 ___ 7 ___ −2 ___ 2 ___ −7
10 ___ T ___ −7 ___ 7 ___ −2 ___ 2 ___ 7 ___ 7 ___ −7
11 ___ T ___ 7 ___ −7 ___ 7 ___ −2 ___ T ___ −7 ___ 7
12 ___ −2 ___ −7 ___ T ___ −7 ___ −7 ___ 7 ___ −2 ___ 7

A7-7
(Copy 4)

Harmonic interval identification: Major and minor seconds, tritones, major and minor sevenths

Shield the answer. Listen to the interval and write 2, −2, T, 7, or −7 in the blank; then uncover the answer and compare your response. Circle incorrect responses. Goal: No more than twelve errors.

1 ___ −2 ___ 2 ___ −7 ___ 7 ___ T ___ −2 ___ −7 ___ T
2 ___ 7 ___ −7 ___ 2 ___ −2 ___ 7 ___ −7 ___ T ___ 2
3 ___ 2 ___ −2 ___ −2 ___ 2 ___ 7 ___ −7 ___ T ___ 7
4 ___ −7 ___ 2 ___ 7 ___ −2 ___ −2 ___ 7 ___ 2 ___ −7
5 ___ −7 ___ 2 ___ 7 ___ −2 ___ 7 ___ −2 ___ 2 ___ −7
6 ___ T ___ −7 ___ −7 ___ 2 ___ 2 ___ −7 ___ 7 ___ −2
7 ___ 7 ___ −2 ___ −2 ___ 7 ___ T ___ −7 ___ T ___ 7
8 ___ −7 ___ 2 ___ 7 ___ −2 ___ 7 ___ −2 ___ −7 ___ 2
9 ___ T ___ −7 ___ T ___ −7 ___ 7 ___ −2 ___ 2 ___ −7
10 ___ T ___ −7 ___ 7 ___ −2 ___ 2 ___ 7 ___ 7 ___ −7
11 ___ T ___ 7 ___ −7 ___ 7 ___ −2 ___ T ___ −7 ___ 7
12 ___ −2 ___ −7 ___ T ___ −7 ___ −7 ___ 7 ___ −2 ___ 7

Harmonic interval identification: Major and minor seconds, tritones, major and minor sevenths

Shield the answer. Listen to the interval and write 2, −2, T, 7, or −7 in the blank; then uncover the answer and compare your response. Circle incorrect responses. Goal: No more than twelve errors.

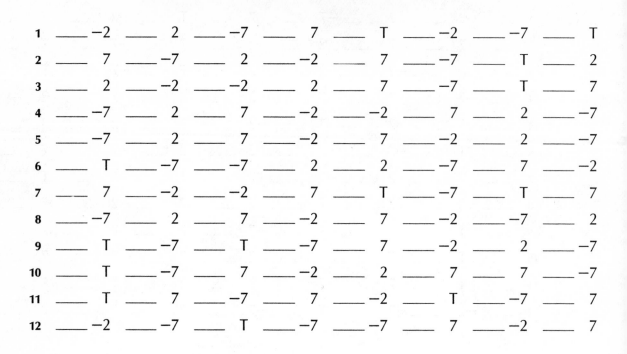

1 ___ −2 ___ 2 ___ −7 ___ 7 ___ T ___ −2 ___ −7 ___ T

2 ___ 7 ___ −7 ___ 2 ___ −2 ___ 7 ___ −7 ___ T ___ 2

3 ___ 2 ___ −2 ___ −2 ___ 2 ___ 7 ___ −7 ___ T ___ 7

4 ___ −7 ___ 2 ___ 7 ___ −2 ___ −2 ___ 7 ___ 2 ___ −7

5 ___ −7 ___ 2 ___ 7 ___ −2 ___ 7 ___ −2 ___ 2 ___ −7

6 ___ T ___ −7 ___ −7 ___ 2 ___ 2 ___ −7 ___ 7 ___ −2

7 ___ 7 ___ −2 ___ −2 ___ 7 ___ T ___ −7 ___ T ___ 7

8 ___ −7 ___ 2 ___ 7 ___ −2 ___ 7 ___ −2 ___ −7 ___ 2

9 ___ T ___ −7 ___ T ___ −7 ___ 7 ___ −2 ___ 2 ___ −7

10 ___ T ___ −7 ___ 7 ___ −2 ___ 2 ___ 7 ___ 7 ___ −7

11 ___ T ___ 7 ___ −7 ___ 7 ___ −2 ___ T ___ −7 ___ 7

12 ___ −2 ___ −7 ___ T ___ −7 ___ −7 ___ 7 ___ −2 ___ 7

A7-8
(Copy 1)

Harmonic interval identification: All intervals previously studied

Shield the answer. Listen to the interval and write the symbol in the blank; then check your response. Circle incorrect responses. Goal: No more than twelve errors. After you have done this lesson, take Test A7.

1 ___ 3 ___ 4 ___ 2 ___ 5 ___ 6 ___ −7 ___ 7 ___ 8

2 ___ 3 ___ −3 ___ 2 ___ 5 ___ 8 ___ 7 ___ 6 ___ 5

3 ___ 2 ___ −3 ___ 3 ___ 4 ___ −2 ___ 2 ___ −3 ___ 3

4 ___ 3 ___ 4 ___ T ___ 5 ___ 6 ___ −6 ___ 7 ___ 8

5 ___ 6 ___ −6 ___ 5 ___ 4 ___ 4 ___ 3 ___ 2 ___ −2

6 ___ 8 ___ 7 ___ −7 ___ 6 ___ 5 ___ 3 ___ −6 ___ −3

7 ___ 3 ___ −3 ___ 5 ___ 7 ___ 5 ___ 3 ___ −3 ___ −7

8 ___ −3 ___ 5 ___ 3 ___ −7 ___ 6 ___ 4 ___ 2 ___ 5

9 ___ 5 ___ −3 ___ 3 ___ −6 ___ −7 ___ 8 ___ 4 ___ 2

10 ___ 8 ___ −7 ___ 3 ___ 5 ___ −3 ___ 3 ___ 6 ___ 8

11 ___ −6 ___ 5 ___ −2 ___ 3 ___ 6 ___ −6 ___ 3 ___ −3

12 ___ −2 ___ 6 ___ T ___ 6 ___ 5 ___ T ___ 6 ___ 3

A7-8
(Copy 2)

Harmonic interval identification: All intervals previously studied

Shield the answer. Listen to the interval and write the symbol in the blank; then check your response. Circle incorrect responses. Goal: No more than twelve errors. After you have done this lesson, take Test A7.

1 ___ 3 ___ 4 ___ 2 ___ 5 ___ 6 ___ −7 ___ 7 ___ 8

2 ___ 3 ___ −3 ___ 2 ___ 5 ___ 8 ___ 7 ___ 6 ___ 5

3 ___ 2 ___ −3 ___ 3 ___ 4 ___ −2 ___ 2 ___ −3 ___ 3

4 ___ 3 ___ 4 ___ T ___ 5 ___ 6 ___ −6 ___ 7 ___ 8

5 ___ 6 ___ −6 ___ 5 ___ 4 ___ 4 ___ 3 ___ 2 ___ −2

6 ___ 8 ___ 7 ___ −7 ___ 6 ___ 5 ___ 3 ___ −6 ___ −3

7 ___ 3 ___ −3 ___ 5 ___ 7 ___ 5 ___ 3 ___ −3 ___ −7

8 ___ −3 ___ 5 ___ 3 ___ −7 ___ 6 ___ 4 ___ 2 ___ 5

9 ___ 5 ___ −3 ___ 3 ___ −6 ___ −7 ___ 8 ___ 4 ___ 2

10 ___ 8 ___ −7 ___ 3 ___ 5 ___ −3 ___ 3 ___ 6 ___ 8

11 ___ −6 ___ 5 ___ −2 ___ 3 ___ 6 ___ −6 ___ 3 ___ −3

12 ___ −2 ___ 6 ___ T ___ 6 ___ 5 ___ T ___ 6 ___ 3

A7-8
(Copy 3)

Harmonic interval identification: All intervals previously studied

Shield the answer. Listen to the interval and write the symbol in the blank; then check your response. Circle incorrect responses. Goal: No more than twelve errors. After you have done this lesson, take Test A7.

1   ___ 3   ___ 4   ___ 2   ___ 5   ___ 6   ___ −7   ___ 7   ___ 8

2   ___ 3   ___ −3   ___ 2   ___ 5   ___ 8   ___ 7   ___ 6   ___ 5

3   ___ 2   ___ −3   ___ 3   ___ 4   ___ −2   ___ 2   ___ −3   ___ 3

4   ___ 3   ___ 4   ___ T   ___ 5   ___ 6   ___ −6   ___ 7   ___ 8

5   ___ 6   ___ −6   ___ 5   ___ 4   ___ 4   ___ 3   ___ 2   ___ −2

6   ___ 8   ___ 7   ___ −7   ___ 6   ___ 5   ___ 3   ___ −6   ___ −3

7   ___ 3   ___ −3   ___ 5   ___ 7   ___ 5   ___ 3   ___ −3   ___ −7

8   ___ −3   ___ 5   ___ 3   ___ −7   ___ 6   ___ 4   ___ 2   ___ 5

9   ___ 5   ___ −3   ___ 3   ___ −6   ___ −7   ___ 8   ___ 4   ___ 2

10   ___ 8   ___ −7   ___ 3   ___ 5   ___ −3   ___ 3   ___ 6   ___ 8

11   ___ −6   ___ 5   ___ −2   ___ 3   ___ 6   ___ −6   ___ 3   ___ −3

12   ___ −2   ___ 6   ___ T   ___ 6   ___ 5   ___ T   ___ 6   ___ 3

A7-8
(Copy 4)

Harmonic interval identification: All intervals previously studied

Shield the answer. Listen to the interval and write the symbol in the blank; then check your response. Circle incorrect responses. Goal: No more than twelve errors. After you have done this lesson, take Test A7.

1   ___ 3   ___ 4   ___ 2   ___ 5   ___ 6   ___ −7   ___ 7   ___ 8

2   ___ 3   ___ −3   ___ 2   ___ 5   ___ 8   ___ 7   ___ 6   ___ 5

3   ___ 2   ___ −3   ___ 3   ___ 4   ___ −2   ___ 2   ___ −3   ___ 3

4   ___ 3   ___ 4   ___ T   ___ 5   ___ 6   ___ −6   ___ 7   ___ 8

5   ___ 6   ___ −6   ___ 5   ___ 4   ___ 4   ___ 3   ___ 2   ___ −2

6   ___ 8   ___ 7   ___ −7   ___ 6   ___ 5   ___ 3   ___ −6   ___ −3

7   ___ 3   ___ −3   ___ 5   ___ 7   ___ 5   ___ 3   ___ −3   ___ −7

8   ___ −3   ___ 5   ___ 3   ___ −7   ___ 6   ___ 4   ___ 2   ___ 5

9   ___ 5   ___ −3   ___ 3   ___ −6   ___ −7   ___ 8   ___ 4   ___ 2

10   ___ 8   ___ −7   ___ 3   ___ 5   ___ −3   ___ 3   ___ 6   ___ 8

11   ___ −6   ___ 5   ___ −2   ___ 3   ___ 6   ___ −6   ___ 3   ___ −3

12   ___ −2   ___ 6   ___ T   ___ 6   ___ 5   ___ T   ___ 6   ___ 3

A7-8

Harmonic interval identification: All intervals previously studied

Shield the answer. Listen to the interval and write the symbol in the blank; then check your response. Circle incorrect responses. Goal: No more than twelve errors. After you have done this lesson, take Test A7.

1. ___ 3 ___ 4 ___ 2 ___ 5 ___ 6 ___ −7 ___ 7 ___ 8
2. ___ 3 ___ −3 ___ 2 ___ 5 ___ 8 ___ 7 ___ 6 ___ 5
3. ___ 2 ___ −3 ___ 3 ___ 4 ___ −2 ___ 2 ___ −3 ___ 3
4. ___ 3 ___ 4 ___ T ___ 5 ___ 6 ___ −6 ___ 7 ___ 8
5. ___ 6 ___ −6 ___ 5 ___ 4 ___ 4 ___ 3 ___ 2 ___ −2
6. ___ 8 ___ 7 ___ −7 ___ 6 ___ 5 ___ 3 ___ −6 ___ −3
7. ___ 3 ___ −3 ___ 5 ___ 7 ___ 5 ___ 3 ___ −3 ___ −7
8. ___ −3 ___ 5 ___ 3 ___ −7 ___ 6 ___ 4 ___ 2 ___ 5
9. ___ 5 ___ −3 ___ 3 ___ −6 ___ −7 ___ 8 ___ 4 ___ 2
10. ___ 8 ___ −7 ___ 3 ___ 5 ___ −3 ___ 3 ___ 6 ___ 8
11. ___ −6 ___ 5 ___ −2 ___ 3 ___ 6 ___ −6 ___ 3 ___ −3
12. ___ −2 ___ 6 ___ T ___ 6 ___ 5 ___ T ___ 6 ___ 3

Test Record Sheet

TEST	MAXIMUM	LEVEL			SCORE AND DATE
		1	2	3	
A2a	250	202	156	109	
A2b	150	121	93	65	
A3a	250	202	156	109	
A3b	150	121	93	65	
A4	400	324	249	174	
A6	400	324	249	174	
A7	400	324	249	174	

All test scores are weighted to compensate for the varying length, difficulty, and importance of the series. The maximum score is the highest attainable score on a test. Level 1 represents high achievement. Level 2 represents moderate or average achievement. Level 3 represents low but significant achievement.

B 0
C 1
D 2
E 3
F 4
G 5
H 6
I 7
J 8
9

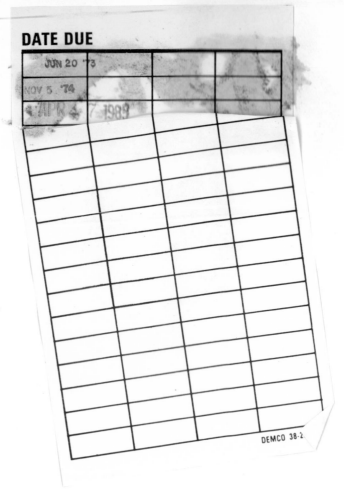